Keeping a Horse at Grass

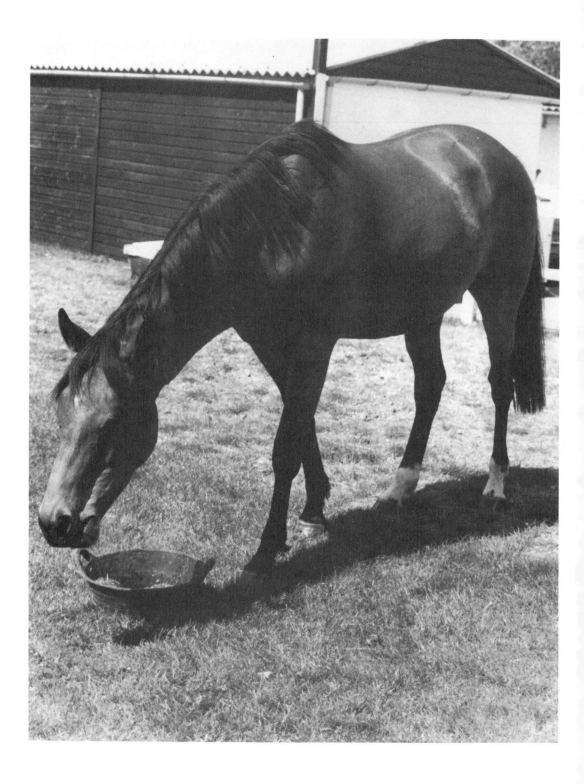

Introduction

While opinions differ on many aspects of horse management, few experts would disagree with the view that it is best to keep horses in an environment that is as near 'natural' as possible for them. For horses, this natural environment means living together with others in a large open space, which has both sufficient shelter and an adequate supply of food and water. However, modern management often dictates that horses are kept stabled, in what amounts to 'solitary confinement' for a large proportion of each 24-hour period, or in the case of many racehorses and valuable competition animals, for all of their time. If this situation were applied to a human being it would be called 'jail', and would therefore be considered intolerable. Why then should it be considered acceptable to keep horses in this way when they are far more gregarious than humans?

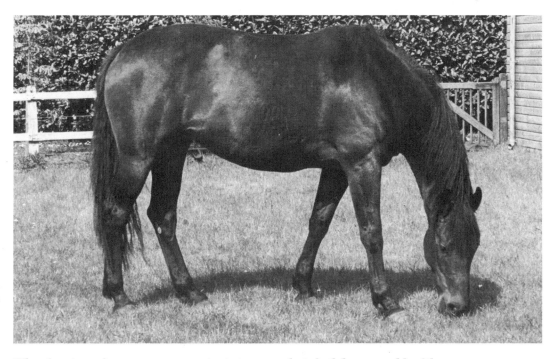

When keeping a horse at grass our aim is to ensure he is both happy and healthy.

Contents

First published in 1995 by
The Crowood Press Ltd
Ramsbury, Marlborough
Wiltshire SN8 2HR

**British Library Cataloguing in
Publication Data**

A catalogue record for this book is available from the
British Library.

ISBN 1 85223 862 3

Photographs by Vanessa Britton
Line-drawings by Rona Knowles

Typeset and designed by:
D & N Publishing
Ramsbury, Marlborough
Wiltshire SN8 2HR

Phototypeset by Dorwyn Ltd, Chichester
Printed and bound at BPC Hazell Books Ltd, Aylesbury

Keeping a Horse
at Grass

VANESSA BRITTON

The Crowood Press

1. Firstly, many people consider that by keeping their horses away from others they are protecting them from being kicked, or infected by others in the field; this is *over-protection*.

2. Secondly, it is more convenient to have horses in stables if they are being worked on a day-to-day basis; this may be true, but the horses will not appreciate the convenience of such an arrangement, so a compromise needs to be made between the time stabled and the time allowed out at grass.

3. Thirdly, many humans tend to give horses human traits, believing they are providing an easier life-style by offering them a nice warm stable with plenty of food; this is a mistake, and such an uneducated view can jeopardize horses' physical and mental health and often amounts to 'killing horses with kindness'.

While most horses are best kept out at grass, there are exceptions, so thankfully, common sense imposes the old rule of treating each horse as an individual. When, for whatever reason, we stable horses, we should remember that we are forcing them to endure conditions that are very unnatural to them. It is true that many horses adapt and seem to cope – but do they really? If this were the case, surely we would not see so many displaying stereotyped behaviour such as weaving and windsucking; after all, wild horses never display such abnormal habits. It may be that some horses 'appear' to cope because they know that after a night in the stable they will be turned out with their companions, and so gain comfort from the familiarity of routine.

You may think this a rather radical view to take, but studies have proved that worry and stress can affect a horse's physical condition, and even predispose him to disease; some monitored horses have developed stomach and intestinal ulcers as a result of such stress. Furthermore, horses that are stabled are unable to relieve any boredom or discomfort they may feel. In the field they can easily roll, pace around, or do whatever they wish to please themselves. In a stable, however, a horse is physically prevented from alleviating the tedium and discomfort and as a result he becomes discontented, and stress follows. Horses experiencing these symptoms have a higher circulation of 'stress' chemicals within their bodies, which interfere with the normal chemical balance of their blood; such horses may then develop behavioural abnormalities of various kinds. It does not require much thought to conclude that it is at best thoughtless, and at worst cruel, to keep horses in an environment which makes them positively miserable.

Obviously, it is of little use to change a horse's environment for one that is just as undesirable. A field should be large enough to provide adequate room for a group of horses to live in harmony with one another. It should provide shelter from both winter and summer elements, and of course, it should be safe.

In producing and maintaining happy, well balanced horses we have to consider what is 'protection' and what is 'over-protection'. It is important to think carefully about individual horses and individual circumstances, and not get trapped within the ideas of 'traditional practice' just because they have dominated the way in which horses have been kept for years. There is no doubt that these traditional ideas are still widely accepted today; but is this because we are doing the best for our horses by keeping them stabled, or because it is the easiest and most convenient arrangement for ourselves?

CHAPTER 1

A Near-Natural Environment

Evolution of the Horse

The most distant relative of the horse is thought to be a small rabbit-like animal known as *Panothere*, which darted about the forest undergrowth like a squirrel. It lived during the Mesozoic period of over 135 million years ago, when humans were also thought to be at the start of their evolutionary pathway. The next stage of equine evolution lies with *Palaeohippus*, about which relatively little is known, as no real evidence of it exists. It was thought to be slightly taller than *Panothere*, which corresponds with the knowledge we have about the horse's early development.

About fifty-five million years ago an animal had developed which some people call the first 'true' ancestor of the horse as we know it today. It was small, about nine inches (23cms) in height, with a short, dumpy neck and eyes that were set to the front of its head. Its unique feature was that it possessed four toes on the front limb, but only three on the hind. It was given the name *Eohippus* or *Hyracotherium*, which means the 'Dawn Horse', and survived by living within the swampy, forested areas typical of the Eocene period. It was not a grazing animal, as horses are today, but a browser of shrubs and undergrowth. Fossil evidence of *Eohippus* is plentiful, both in Europe and North America, which were at that time connected by land.

The tropical, forested environment at the time developed into extensive grassy

Eohippus saw significant climatic and environmental changes, which meant it had to adapt in order to survive. Many subscribe to the theory that the horse developed certain characteristics in order to cope with environmental change, believing that the evolution of animals is concomitant with environmental mutation. Generally, however, this is considered to be not strictly true, and many feel that it was simply a matter of chance that the horse survived, believing that some just happened to have developed the characteristics that allowed them to continue to exist, and not that such development was inevitable. This theory is borne out by the fact that many other ancestral lines relating to the horse did become extinct due to their inability to cope with the new environment.

One of the most pleasing sights of social behaviour is that of two horses grooming each other, as both derive immense pleasure from this activity.

Eohippus *or the 'Dawn Horse' first appeared on earth some 55 million years ago.*

plains and so *Eohippus* had to learn to graze, rather than browse for food in order to survive. New, more life-threatening predators were also evolving, and as a result it developed an efficient defence system known today as the 'flight reflex' which enabled it to run swiftly from predators at a moment's warning. Consequently, or perhaps by chance, the horse evolved into a successful herbivore that was capable of protecting itself by rapidly distancing itself from any threatening situation.

As the years went by the horse's body went through some remarkable changes, until it became the horse we know today. The most significant of these was a general increase in size: from being no bigger than a rabbit, the horse developed until it reached the size of the modern-day horse. This larger frame provided more room for a bigger heart and lungs, which was necessary for sudden and swift retreats, and there was also more space for the more complicated digestive system that was necessary to deal with the greater masses of grass consumed from its new surroundings. The horse's limb bones lengthened and strengthened, providing the ability to move at much greater speed, necessary for a hasty retreat. The head and neck became longer so that the horse could graze at floor level, and the eyes moved round to the sides of the head to facilitate all-round vision. It took more than sixty million years for it to develop in this way, and it was not until about one million years ago that *Equus* appeared, the direct antecedent of today's horse.

At one time it was thought that the species *Equus caballus* (the domesticated horse) came from one single source, but it has since been recognized that several wild species contributed to its make-up. The horse became widely disseminated as herds migrated to other continents, with representatives such as Przewalski's horse, the zebra and the African wild ass still surviving today. Interbreeding must have occurred between these ancient types, resulting in the breeds that we recognize today, such as the Shire horse, British native ponies and notably the Arab. Selective breeding by humans brought about the Thoroughbred, which largely descends from crossbreeds of three Arabian stallions: the Godolphin, the Darley Arabian and the Byerley Turk. These stallions also had a profound effect on other breeds, and with the resulting crossbreeding that went on, hundreds of 'types' emerged. How the Arab itself originated is unclear, but its characteristics certainly set it apart from others of its kind.

Domestication

The value of the pre-domestic horse to ancient man was initially in terms of its meat and hide. He also used horses for sacrificial purposes, often accumulating huge piles of their bones outside his cave in order to ward off evil, and their dung was employed as a fuel source. While at first horses must obviously have been hunted and killed on the spot, we know from cave paintings that at some point they were trapped and kept alive in order to provide fresh meat and clothes, without the need to hunt for them each day. This must have taken a great deal of cunning on the trapper's part, because until its domestication the horse's chief enemy was man.

The domestication of the horse is thought to have taken place some 5,000 years ago, although there is no clear evidence to support this assumption. Horses were first put to domestic use as a means of pulling heavy things, including people in primitive vehicles such as sledges, and of course the ancient Egyptians and Greeks are renowned for their particular mode of transport, the chariot. At some point though, whether by chance or intention, the horse came to be employed as a personal means of transport, the role he holds in modern-day times, where he is mainly kept for riding.

When dealing with horses, even ones that have been a domestic breed for hundreds of years, we must never lose sight of their instinctive behaviour. Although they are now almost entirely domesticated, they are still born with the natural instincts of their predecessors who had to defend themselves against predators and survive despite a constantly changing world. The modern horse still displays many of the characteristics which its

> Today's horse is very much an animal of pleasure and recreation: through him, many of us are able to participate in the great variety of equestrian sports that are available. However, while he is a willing and faithful companion, for his own well-being we must also allow him to be what he really is, a herd animal. Living in harmony together is the aim, to which the key is satisfying each other's needs.

The modern horse still displays many of the characteristics its ancient ancestors possessed millions of years ago.

ancient ancestors possessed millions of years ago. Thus an understanding of the horse's evolution should have a significant influence on the way in which we manage him in current times; so that we may satisfy his basic needs and acknowledge what his 'natural' behaviour really is.

As a result of domestication the horse has certainly lost out in many respects, but he has also gained a great deal. Living a natural life may entail having the run of open countryside, roaming grassy plains and valleys, taking water from cool, running streams, dozing under a belt of shady trees and breeding freely; but it also entails the possibility of an early death from illness, injury, starvation, thirst and enemies. We tend to imagine that the horse's agrarian environment is rather idyllic, but what happens when things turn rough – when grazing supplies diminish due to poor weather; when it is bitterly cold, with driving wind and rain; when any natural water supply either dries up, becomes polluted or freezes over; when a particular individual is ostracized from the herd, simply because he or she is deemed to pose a threat? At such times, surely the horse is glad to be a domesticated animal, that knows his human companion will come to the rescue?

In order that the mutually rewarding relationship between horse and human flourishes, we must first examine our usual management methods, evaluating the horse's genuine needs as defined by nature and his own progressive development. Then we must look at what we expect of the horse in return, and only then can we begin to devise a better way of keeping him within the constraints of the resources available to us.

Environmental Effects

The horse has proved to be a remarkably adaptable animal. When his environment changed, he also changed and thus survived where others perished. As the horse species expanded and went its different ways, so each distinct herd learned to exist, and indeed thrive, in the widely varying climatic conditions in which it found itself all over the world. However, it is important to understand, that it is because these horses developed in such a way as to equip them to survive in their given environment that they did so; other lines that were not sufficiently well developed perished. Whether the evolution of the horse was a matter of adapting to a changing environment, or of sheer chance will always be cause for debate, but it does

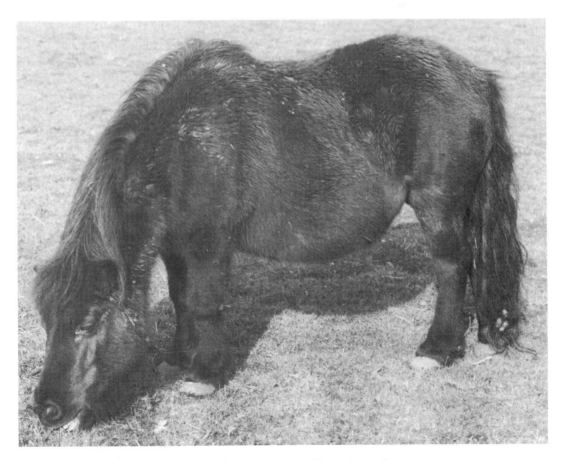

The horse or pony is an animal that functions most efficiently in the environment in which it developed; the Shetland pony thrives best in the Shetland Isles, for instance.

Keeping a horse at grass takes just as much thought as keeping one in a stable; it is not an easy option that enables you to turn your horse out and forget about him. The importance of his environment is just as significant as his basic needs of survival, and so a totally holistic approach should be employed. Consider the horse as an animal that functions most efficiently in the environment in which it has developed: thus the New Forest pony thrives best in the New Forest; the Arab horse in Arabia and so on. In order to grasp this concept fully it is necessary to take it to extremes: consider how long a shark would survive on a beach without water, or how long we would survive in the ocean.

not directly affect the modern day horse-owner. All we must do is to ensure that the horse we have is either naturally suited to the environment he lives in, or is provided with alternative means which will enable him to cope with his surroundings. It will be obvious to most people that if the Thoroughbred were left to roam the Yorkshire Dales in the United Kingdom, it would not thrive, or survive for very long as a breed.

Horses differ greatly in their ability to cope with various environments; even if they were provided with a very gradual acclimatization period, some may still never adapt properly to one which is totally different from that in which they evolved. Obviously then, each breed has an optimum environment which has loosely set limits. Provide the horse with an optimum environment and his body will work at its most effective; but the further you push him outside the limits of his optimum environment, the less efficient he will be at maintaining himself. This results in more input being required from

us in order to try and compensate for his hardship: more feed, more shelter, more time and more expense!

The Hierarchy System

In a natural setting, herd life for the horse is matriarchal: the leader of the herd is a mare, not a stallion as is often thought. This one mare alone dictates where the herd goes and generally makes all the major decisions. The female members of a herd are usually quite strongly bonded together; each has her place, commonly dictated by age, and as long as she remembers it there are few problems.

The role of the stallion is purely to mate with the mares, and to keep his 'harem' intact; he will fight for it, but does not usually take charge of the day to day order of things. Colt foals are accepted in the herd until they become sexually active, at which time the stallion usually decides that they will soon pose a threat to his supremacy and so chases them out. These young colts will often band together into a bachelor group, until they are old enough each to form a herd of his own. Females are gathered in a number of ways:
• Females may decide to leave the main herd voluntarily and join with the young male, perhaps desiring to be the matriarch themselves;
• Young fillies may be ousted from the herd by the main stallion if he feels he already has a large enough number of females to cope with;
• A bachelor stallion may steal them from the main herd, which may involve a fight.

Horses are capable of reproducing very early on in their lives; a two year old filly can quite easily be successfully mated by a yearling colt, for instance. However,

Herd life is matriarchal; this means that the leader of the herd is a mare and she will do everything within her power to protect her own young and the herd.

Horse-play can often seem quite aggressive to the onlooker, but is usually quite harmless.

while domesticated broodmares are usually put 'in foal' each year, the feral mare does not always produce a foal annually. Wild mares also stop breeding at a younger age, usually around fifteen, whereas healthy broodmares of twenty plus are not uncommon on studs. The domesticated horse's lifespan is between twenty-five to twenty-eight years of age, which is quite a bit longer than that of the feral horse, whose lifespan is governed by his health and teeth, an older horse's teeth can deteriorate quite rapidly until he reaches a point when he can simply no longer eat. In the wild he would perish, but our older horses stay alive for longer because their teeth are cared for throughout their lives, and because we feed them soft, easily chewed food if necessary.

Social Behaviour

Horses have clearly defined rules within their society and as long as a young horse is allowed to associate with others, whether in a domestic or wild state, he will learn what is required of him. Horses live in this way because it is natural to their survival, a lone animal is at great

A young horse showing her dominance over an 'underling', in this case a sheep!

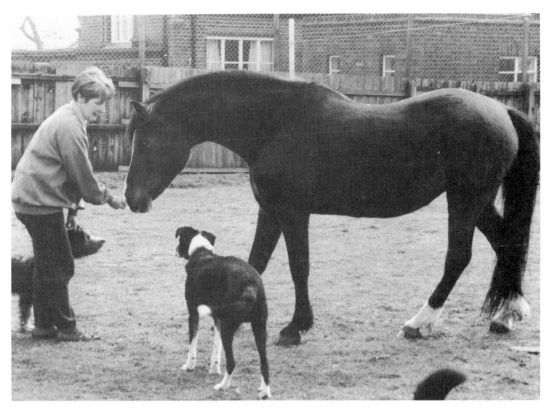

If there are no other horses around a horse will try to form a herd with other 'animals'.

risk from predators, whereas in a group situation there is a far higher degree of safety. This is why a young colt disinherited from the herd will find others in the same predicament to form a bachelor band, or may join with older, dispossessed stallions until he can form his own herd: it is the maxim of 'safety in numbers'.

Obviously domesticated horses are not at risk from predators, but the instincts are still there. When a number of horses are put together in a domestic situation, they will still form a 'pecking order'. It need not necessarily be the oldest mare that heads the band, but generally youngsters are more subservient. Left to their own devices horses will sort themselves out, and while there may be a few squabbles at first, horses rarely suffer great injuries. In fact, more harm can be done by keeping a horse away from his companions because we fear the risk of injury, as he can suffer great psychological stress. Where horses are turned out together as a daily part of their routine, injuries rarely occur whether the horses are shod or not; it is introducing a new member to an established group which may cause problems (see Chapter 2). For the risk of a slight injury during play, it

In the interests of safety it is important that all horses that are turned out together are congenial towards each other.

really is not worth jeopardizing the horse's contentment by keeping him on his own.

In order to form natural social bonds with their companions, horses must be allowed to touch and communicate with each other freely. Horses can and do form close friendships with each other, usually with those of an equal standing in the herd. When stabling horses, this friendship should be preserved by housing the horses next to each other. Often people will separate horses because they cannot manage one while his friend is around; however, this is simply a failure on the owner's part to teach the horse good manners and respect. Once a horse realizes that he will be reunited with his friend after he has carried out whatever task is required of him, he will work willingly. Trying to separate them will simply result in them fretting, so they will not be able to concentrate properly on the job in hand anyway.

While out in the field, each horse has his own 'personal space'; family members and close friends will be allowed to enter this space, but others will not. You may have heard someone saying 'those two don't like each other' when referring to two particular horses. This is quite natural between two horses that are not closely bonded; but it is not so much dislike as merely not needing each other's company.

Sometimes it will satisfy a more dominant horse if the subordinate one moves away upon his arrival. As an example, take the underling who is dozing under a tree: when he sees the group leader approach in desire of his spot, he will move away without question. However, if a horse of only slightly higher rank approaches he may need to be told to move on by a threatening look and possibly a nip. And when a horse of equal rank approaches, there may be a stand-up fight, and this is when injuries can occur. Fortunately horses are rarely vicious, but you do need to keep a watchful eye on a group of horses grazing together. One of the most pleasing sights of social behaviour is that of two horses grooming each other, as both derive immense pleasure from this activity.

If feeling particularly relaxed and unthreatened, two compatible horses will lie down side by side.

When we turn horses out together it is our job to ensure they enjoy their time at liberty. This comes from ensuring that all those turned out together are congenial towards each other. While the nature of herd life is to have some horses more dominant than others, unfortunately you can also get individuals that are just plain bullies; this results in subordinate horses being constantly driven away from the rest of the group, and generally deprived of their right to peace when grazing, drinking or dozing. It is bad management to allow such a situation to develop, and plain stupidity to allow it to continue: it is the bully horse that needs to be removed from the herd, not the underlings.

Spend a little time watching a group of horses at liberty, and you will find it fascinating. There are many things they will do for each other as well as grooming, such as swatting flies off one another's face with their tails, or standing guard over a companion who is lying down; and if they are feeling particularly relaxed they will both lie down together.

The Horse's Senses

The horse has five main senses, which are those of seeing, hearing, tasting, touching and smelling. It can also be justified that the horse has a 'sixth sense', an unknown quality which causes him to react to what is happening around him, without there being anything physical to substantiate his feelings and subsequent reactions. For instance, he can often tell whether his owner is in a particularly sad or happy frame of mind; he 'knows', yet he cannot ask them if this is so.

Sight

The horse has an exceptionally wide field of vision, achieved because his eyes are set high up on the side of his head, rather than to the front. He can see to the front with both eyes (binocular vision), and on each side with each individual eye (monocular vision). This means that he is able to see anything approaching from the rear, even with his head still down while grazing; should something then take his interest, he will often look around in order to scrutinize it further by concentrating both eyes upon it. Moreover there are certain mechanisms in the horse's eyes, which lead us to believe that he is a nocturnal animal: firstly, many of you will have seen how they glow in the dark; and secondly, a horse is able to find his way around without daylight due to a light-enhancing surface within the eye that reflects as much light as is available back onto the retina. However, the horse's eyes adjust quite slowly to changes in light, which is why many of them are hesitant when entering a horsebox, or when jumping from light into dark.

It is often said that the vision of a wall-eyed horse is limited, and that he is likely to be skittish and quick-tempered. There is no evidence to substantiate this claim, and a wall-eyed horse is no more likely to be at a disadvantage when living out at grass than any other horse.

Unlike our own, the horse's eye has the ability to focus on both near and far objects at the same time. The benefit of this to the horse is obviously of extreme importance, for not only can he see what he is eating but he can also see exactly who, or what is approaching! However, he does have a blind spot directly in front of and behind him, extending to about four feet (120cm) away from his face; this is why you should not approach a horse from directly in front or behind. In addition, his muzzle obscures anything directly below his eyes to floor level, the effects of which you might observe when he bangs his

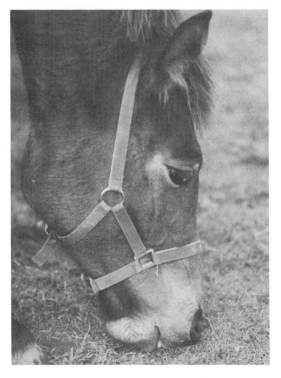

The horse has the ability to rotate his ears through 360 degrees. This enables him to hear what is going on all around him without having to raise his head or move his body in any way.

muzzle on a fence post or other object directly below his face.

Hearing

The horse's sense of hearing is very well developed. In order that he can hear sounds from any direction, each ear can move independently of the other, having the ability to rotate through 360 degrees; this enables him to hear what is going on all around him without having to raise his head or move his body in any way. Moreover, the horse's detection of tonal range is far greater than our own, extending from very low to extremely high frequencies. This ability to recognize a large tonal range can work to our advantage: thus a long and low sound soothes the horse, while a short, higher pitched tone can act as a reprimand. Young horses quickly

Take care not to expose the horse to a constantly noisy environment as his hearing is sensitive. What is simply 'busy' noise to us may appear chaotic to him, and what is loud to us may appear to him to be almost deafening. Sudden noises will upset a horse, and while *Radio One* may chivvy along those who are mucking out, it is simply another nuisance for the domesticated horse to contend with.

Once a horse has detected a sound he will look up in its direction, pricking his ears towards it.

learn to respond to their name if it is said in the same manner each time, which can be of great benefit when trying to catch a horse in a hurry or even in the dark!

A horse's hearing is far more acute than our own: once he has detected a sound he will look up in its direction, pricking his ears towards it. You may not be able to see what it is he can hear, but undoubtedly whatever it is he has detected will soon appear.

Smell

A good sense of smell is one of the horse's greatest assets: it helps a mare to detect and bond with her foal; it tells a stallion when a mare is ready for mating; it is a means of identifying others, humans as well as equine; and coupled with the sense of taste, it also helps the horse avoid eating poisonous plants. In the wild it will help him to detect the approach of predators from quite a distance, and even watering holes can be smelt from far away.

Whenever a horse approaches something strange the first thing he will do is to flare his nostrils and sniff in order to get a

The horse's sense of smell is one that can work against us. How many times have you tried to give your horse a worming powder or some other additive in his feed only to find that he instantly detects and rejects it? This can be overcome either by trying to disguise the additive with another more pleasantly smelling one, such as molasses or menthol, or by putting the same onto the horse's muzzle to confuse him and perhaps therefore duping him into eating it.

good smell of it. Two unacquainted horses will also use the same techniques, blowing gently into each other's nostrils; and if one or other does not like what he smells a squeal, nip or a kick may swiftly follow.

Taste

Horses have a very good sense of taste, in that they are able to detect what is palatable from the first bite, discarding anything less desirable from the mouth that has fooled the sense of smell. The four qualities recognized by the horse are the same as the ones we know: sweet, sour, bitter and salty. The horse's preference is usually for sweet or salty things, but the others also have an appeal and what may seem quite bitter to us, can genuinely seem quite nice to the horse. Horses found to be fussy eaters may have a very delicate sense of taste, and often a change of brand or the addition of something pleasant may be enough to encourage a horse to eat up well. The time to be concerned is if a horse that normally eats well suddenly stops doing so. Many poisonous plants are bitter to the horse and unless he is extremely hungry he will reject them. However, such plants can lose their bitterness when baled into hay, so always be on the lookout out for this.

Touch

Even though the horse has a hairy coat, his sense of touch is just as acute as our own. To be more precise perhaps we should talk in terms of 'feel', in that the horse can feel touch, pressure, pain, hot and cold. He knows the instant a fly lands on him, and will feel pain or pleasurable sensations just as intently as we do. In order to 'touch' objects, the horse uses his muzzle in the same way that we use our

> Always bear in mind the horse's sensitivity to touch, and remember that a great big slap on the neck is not a caress masked by the word 'pat', but a smack! Be gentle with the horse and judge how he feels pressure and sensation by your own sensitivity to such things.

fingers. He will run his muzzle over them, and generally investigate by engaging his nostrils, lips and tongue. He feels hot and cold as we do, and is just as sensitive to textures as we are. Many people often wonder as to the purpose of a horse's whiskers, and simply cut them off in order to improve his appearance without due regard to their function, but horse's whiskers enable him to judge the proximity of close objects. We have already seen how he is unable to see below his eyes, or directly in front of him, and it is his whiskers that provide this service for him.

Sixth Sense

As discussed, 'sixth sense' is something beyond comprehension, and may therefore be sneered at by some people. Whatever the arguments for and against, it is undoubtedly true that horses can detect things which we cannot. Possibly this ability is linked to the the fact that the horse's other highly tuned senses are acting in harmony, but nevertheless, not all can be explained. Why is it that horses seem to be able to detect approaching weather? Similarly, some have been known to refuse point blank to go near radioactive material, and many of us who have been around horses a long time will know that whatever the critics say, our own horses do seem to react to our own moods. It is often said that certain people simply have 'a way with horses' and this can perhaps be explained by the idea that they are receptive to each other's thought patterns; they are on the same wavelength, if you like.

While there is still much about horses that is not comprehended, we do know that they quickly learn to associate one experience with another. The man smelling of antiseptic almost always brings with him a big needle; putting on a headcollar in the morning means being turned out; being plaited means going to a show and a silent owner with no sugar lumps means that he or she has got the hump! Thus, not everything we assign to the horse's sixth sense is past understanding, but there is still a lot to learn.

CHAPTER 2

The 'Ideal' Outdoor Horse

What Type of Horse Thrives Outdoors?

In order to answer this question we need to assess just what the domesticated horse's fundamental needs are. In Chapter 1 we saw how deep-rooted his inherent characteristics are. In a time scale of years, we have had an association with the horse for a relatively short period; we cannot therefore expect that the horse would further develop in order to adapt to our needs. Nothing we do is going to alter significantly the characteristics of the horse, and the more we try to alter things towards our own convenience the more problems we will encounter along the way. However, we must also remember that many horses have been selectively bred by man, and although they still have the inborn characteristics of their species, their physical needs will to some extent be dictated by what we have made them.

When considering whether a horse is a suitable candidate for outdoor living we should assess whether the living conditions we propose to offer him will provide everything he needs.

• **Food** Horses are trickle feeders, which means they require an almost constant turnover of food in order to keep their digestive system working properly. Keeping a horse in a field obviously satisfies this need as long as there is an adequate supply of grass. However, this 'at grass' lifestyle does not suit all horses and ponies. Take the Shetland pony, for instance. If he is allowed to graze *ad libitum* on good spring grass, there is a fair chance he will end up suffering from laminitis (see Chapter 9). This is because in his natural setting he would have to travel considerable distances in order to consume enough of the poor nutritional forage sparsely offered on the Shetland Isles, in order to maintain himself. This being his optimum environment, it is not surprising that he can suffer when translocated to a field setting where he is offered an effortless feast. By comparison, the Thoroughbred horse may not thrive at all at grass, requiring extra nutrition in order to keep him in good condition. Obviously then we must firstly think about the breed and type of horse we have.

• **Exercise** This is essential to the physical and mental health of all horses. While turned out the horse can exercise himself as he would naturally, by wandering round the paddock in order to gaze, and by playing with his companions. The horse is an animal of a number of paces, all of which were designed to be employed. In order to maintain physical health the horse must be able to extend his body and limbs throughout all his paces whatever his age. Study a horse in his natural setting and you will see all his paces being utilized quite frequently. Where a horse is stabled the best we can offer is long rides away from his life of confinement, but this is still a poor substitute

While turned out the horse can exercise himself as he would naturally, by wandering round the paddock in order to graze, and by playing with his companions.

Where a paddock is not available, a more appropriate alternative to stabling is 'yarding'.

Horses are gregarious animals, which means they like the company of others.

In the wild, horses would find large trees to shelter under, away from driving rain or the constant irritation of flies.

for complete freedom where he can exercise when and how he so desires. Where a paddock is not available, a more appropriate alternative to stabling is 'yarding'. This is where the horse has a large pen to roam about in, and although he cannot trot or canter, at least he is not confined to looking at four solid walls.

• **Company** Horses are gregarious animals, which means they like to be sociable with others. Apart from the survival instinct of safety in numbers, feral horses live in herds because they actually enjoy each other's company. Depriving a young horse of the company of others can leave psychological scars which may

never be conquered, no matter how many companions the horse is provided with in subsequent years. Young foals especially do not seem to relate properly to others of their species later in life and also appear to have a lack of common 'horse' sense. It is rather like depriving a young child of his nursery education, only to put him straight into senior school; obviously he would be totally out of his depth, and perhaps unable ever to catch up.

• **Shelter** All horses need shelter from both winter and summer elements. In the wild they would find large trees to shelter under, away from driving rain or the constant irritation of flies. If a horse paddock does not have any form of weather shield it must be provided with one by erecting a field shelter (see Chapter 3).

• **Warmth** This is closely related to food and shelter, and all a native horse may require is that his coat is allowed to grow naturally in relation to the climate. If the horse is a finer breed, or has had his coat clipped while in work, then he will need extra clothing, and possibly food too in order to maintain his body heat during cold weather.

By understanding these basic needs we will begin to realize that the closer we keep to what nature has provided, the fewer problems we will create for both ourselves and our horses.

Considerations for Outdoor Living

Age

Age is not a major consideration for the horse living outdoors, until he becomes very old. Other than a Thoroughbred or finely bred horse, and unless human intervention has brought their birth date much earlier in the year, many foals can live out from the moment they are born. Older horses may be at slightly more risk, needing more food and rugs, but nevertheless being left to roam about freely does help to prevent them from becoming too stiff. Common sense should prevail, but as long as the horse is otherwise healthy and has all his basic needs provided, there is little need to stable him more as he gets older. A very old horse may be an exception, as his heating mechanism may not be quite what it should be. However, in this situation you still need to weigh up the advantages and disadvantages because an old horse that has lived

out all his life might start to fret if suddenly stabled; so in this case you should consider whether providing more rugs, food and shelter might be a better solution.

Breeding

The horse's breeding matters a great deal when considering how it is best kept. Not only is this dictated by what breed he is, but also by the characteristics inherited through his parents. It is well known that a native horse will live out all year round with fewer problems than a full Thoroughbred. Yet what is not so widely known is that a native mare or stallion that has an aversion to cold weather, or biting flies because it is thin-skinned, can pass on this trait to its progeny, too. As a foal receives half its genes (hereditary instructions) from its dam and half from its sire, it has a fifty-fifty chance of possessing such characteristics. It all depends whether the particular gene for a certain trait is dominant or recessive; for example if the foal displays the temperament and colour of its dam, then these genes were obviously dominant over the stallion's. This is why it is always worth spending some time studying the dam and stallion of any foal, or proposed breeding stock, so that you can weigh up the suitability of the horse for living outdoors. Where both sire and dam seem to be well suited to outdoor living, the resulting foal should also be, although of course there will always be the exception to the rule.

Temperament

Temperament is important when considering a horse's suitability for living out of doors. First, he has to be a contented type that is not continually looking to come in.

Some horses are not suited to living outdoors so problems such as crib-biting can develop; usually these horses have had a heavily competitive life and simply do not want to be retired.

Certainly many horses will stand at the gate at feed times, but this is quite different from the horse that constantly walks up and down the fence or crib-bites until he is brought in. Such horses may be used to a competitive life with constant attention from their rider and groom, travelling a great deal and generally enjoying a very busy schedule. Others simply seem to prefer life 'indoors', but they are few and far between. Horses that do walk the fence can be extremely difficult to maintain in good condition, and once this behavioural pattern has developed it is almost impossible to break it, no matter how many companions the horse has with him.

Horses that are highly strung are also poor choices for outdoor living as they may not keep weight on easily and may generally fail to thrive. On the other hand, should their unrestful nature be due to being kept in a stable for most of their time, then obviously being turned out is going to provide a solution. Assessing the horse is really a matter of common sense coupled with some understanding of each individual horse's make-up.

When considering temperament you must also give thought to how your horse views others of his own kind. Is he the dominant or the subordinate type? You can only assess this by observing his reaction to others when in company. It does not automatically follow that a horse which is pushy towards humans, will intimidate other horses; he may in fact be quite slavish. Similarly, a placid, well-tempered horse around humans may well be the 'boss' when out in the field. Having deduced what type of horse you have, take measures to ensure that he is only turned out with those with which he is compatible.

Rigs

One type of horse that can be a real nuisance in the field is a rig, a gelding that thinks and behaves like a stallion. When mares are in season he may fight with other horses, and can even be very protective over other geldings. At such times he may also be rather less than co-operative with you. So what makes a horse a rig, and what can be done about it?

A rig is technically known as a *cryptorchid*, where either one or both of the testes have failed to drop down into the scrotal sac so that normal 'stallion' hormones are still produced, so naturally the horse acts as though he is still a stallion. A rig is not fertile because any testis which does not reach the scrotum is not able to produce sperm. However, should only one be retained, then on maturity the testicle which has descended will produce fertile sperm and is therefore capable of putting a mare into foal. Such a horse must obviously not be kept in a field with mares, and to all intents and purposes will need to be managed as a stallion.

Some geldings may act like stallions even though they have been correctly castrated, both their testicles having been removed. These are known as *'false' rigs* and they can demonstrate very masculine behaviour, from simply rounding up a group of mares, to full penetration of a mare. It used to be thought that such horses had not been properly castrated, but this is now known not to be the case. It would appear that such horses behave as they do simply because of inborn instincts that have not been suppressed by castration, as usually happens. There is no effective treatment for this type of horse although his macho behaviour may lessen as he matures.

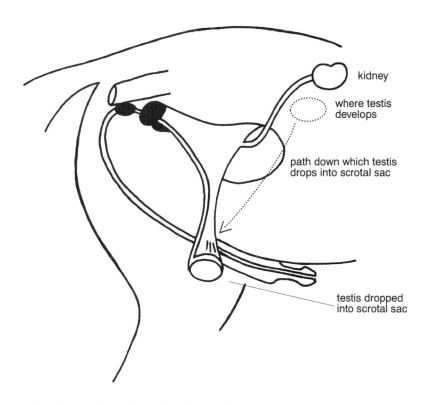

Where the testes develop and how they should drop into the scrotal sac.

If you are worried that your horse may be a rig, either because you have no history of his castration or because he is exhibiting stallion behaviour, you should ask your vet to check him for you. He or she will examine your horse to see if there is any physical evidence of a testis, although in fact the only positive method of detection is by a blood test. A horse can now be tested for being a rig from as young as two years of age. If the test is positive your vet will advise on suitable castration methods, which will require a general anaesthetic in order to locate the retained testis. However, vets do consider this to be a routine operation, with little more risk than any other that involves putting the horse under general anaesthetic. Even if a true rig does not display any aggressive behaviour towards you or his field companions, in the interests of safety and perhaps unwanted pregnancies in the future, he should still be castrated.

Do not be tempted to use a rig for breeding purposes. Cryptorchidism is an hereditary imperfection and no breed society would ever consider issuing a licence for such a horse as the defect can only be eliminated by selective breeding.

To thrive outdoors a horse must be in good physical health,
and this includes condition.

Health

To thrive outdoors a horse must be in good physical health, and this includes the condition he is carrying. Thus a thin horse may feel the cold easily, whereas a fatter one might actually suffer from being exposed to too much feed. Your horse's ribs should be reasonably well covered, but not to the extreme that he appears fat and dreary – if he is too fat, he will be just as much at risk to health problems as if he is too thin. Run your fingers along his rib cage: you should just be able to feel them (see Chapter 7 for more information).

The important thing is that you learn to recognize what constitutes 'normal' for your horse. If you do not know him that well you will be slow to pick up on the little tell-tale signs which might otherwise have warned you that he was ailing. Take time each day to have a good look at your horse in the field, and give him a health check frequently as a form of preventive medicine.

Many owners know their horses so well that they can tell if they are 'off colour' by just looking at them. In such cases a physical examination will confirm what they already suspect.

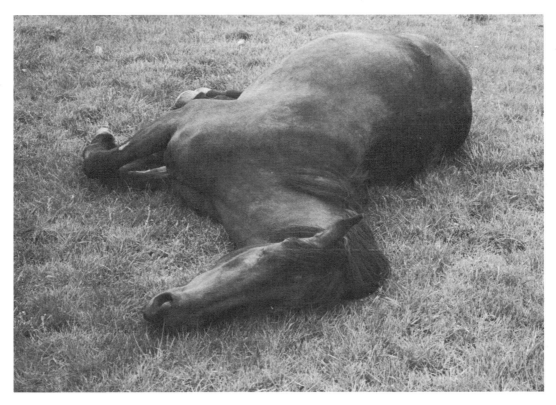

This horse is literally 'fast asleep'. Against popular belief, many horses will continue to lie down in your presence, only reluctantly getting up if you give them a stern enough prod!

Observing the Field-Kept Horse

The healthy horse should always appear bright and cheerful. Your particular horse may have his own idiosyncrasies, but he should never appear 'sick or sorry'. Alertness is a good indicator of health, so check that your horse is looking to see what is going on around him, or looks up when you approach: if he usually whickers when he sees you, take note if one day he does not. Before going to catch your horse notice where he is in the field: if he is looking dejected and is on his own, or shows any other unusual behaviour, then some sort of illness may be brewing. Always double check if you are unsure by carrying out some physical tests (see next section).

Always be on the lookout for potential problems so they can be confronted and resolved in as short a time as possible. Although living out of doors is natural for the horse, it does not mean that he can look after himself; the horse is still dependant on us for his needs and this includes his health.

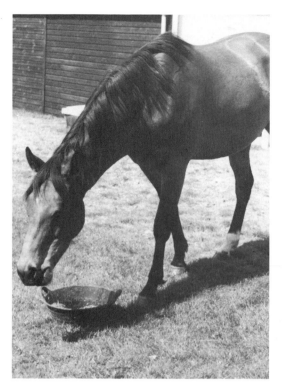

If you notice that your horse is quidding, he may have a problem with his teeth; this needs immediate attention before his health starts to suffer as a result.

glossy sheen to his coat. His natural oils will keep his skin and coat in good condition, even if you do not have the time to groom him every day. However, flaky, scurfy skin may mean there is some underlying problem, and this should be investigated.

Appetite is one of the first things to be affected if your horse is feeling off-colour so watch to see whether he is grazing normally. Unless you know him to be a fussy eater he should eat up well. Food left in a feed tub in the field should set your warning bells ringing, unless perhaps your horse has had a recent change of environment; being turned out into a lush paddock when previously he was on a sparse one, for instance. Should he suddenly develop a poor appetite it is often a warning that colic or some sort of viral infection is imminent. And notice if your horse frequently drops food from his mouth (known as quidding), this may indicate that he has a problem with his teeth, and needs immediate attention before his health starts to suffer as a result.

When observing any horse in the field, look to see how he is standing. The healthy horse will stand evenly on all four feet, or might rest a hind foot if he is feeling particularly relaxed. Horses can sleep standing up, but will lie down in the field if they do not feel threatened at all. Many people will tell you that a horse should jump up as you approach. However, this is simply not the case, and many horses will remain lying down, only getting up reluctantly given a stern enough prod!

Unless living out without a rug in the winter your horse should have a nice

Physical Examination

Whenever you visit your horse first thing in the morning, check him all over to make sure he has come through the night unscathed. First, just look him quickly all over to ensure he has no cuts or swellings or foreign objects imbedded in his skin. Then take a closer look at him:
• His eyes should be bright and focused, and the eye membranes should be a nice salmon pink colour. However, it is important to check these while your horse is in good health, as some horses have naturally paler membranes than others.
• While at rest your horse's respiration

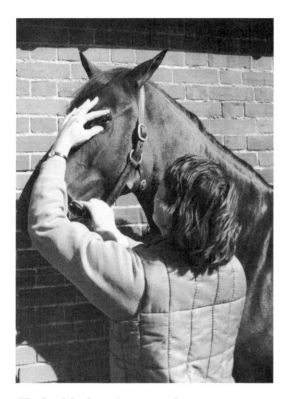

The healthy horse's eye membranes should be a nice salmon-pink colour.

rate should be between eight and twelve breaths per minute and they should be even and regular.

Maintaining Good Health

While it is all very well to have the horse treated when things go wrong, it is far better if you can prevent problems from occurring in the first place. As the owner of a horse you have certain responsibilities to uphold, in order that he is cared for in the best possible way.

• You should provide your horse with a balanced diet, the amount relating to the exercise he receives, his size and

Limitations of a Grass-Kept Horse

It is often thought that a grass-kept horse will not have the same ability to perform as a stable kept one. This is a fallacy. It is undoubtedly more convenient to compete with the stable kept horse, as he is always on hand, and usually clean when you need him. However, providing the grass kept horse is well cared for there will be no difference between his stamina and ability than that of his stabled companion. In fact, it is often an advantage to compete the horse from the field as he will be quite relaxed and loose throughout his body, whereas a stabled horse may need more warming up before any real work can begin.

Obviously there are drawbacks for the owner. You cannot ride the horse whenever you like as he may be wet, or extremely muddy. You could bring your horse in to dry him off first, but you may simply not have the time to do this. You may find it is more difficult to keep your horse's coat in good order; other horses may chew or bite it, which does not look too good if you are intending to show or do dressage. However, there are few problems that cannot be overcome. Often a combined system works well for horses that are regularly competing. Either they are kept in at nights and turned out during the day, or just kept in the day before a show.

metabolism. Also remember that the climate can dictate the need for more or less feed.

• You should ensure he receives basic routine care such as regular worming, vaccinations, foot care and dentistry. As a general rule horses need worming every six to eight weeks, although this does depend on certain individual factors such as whether your horse is in a large

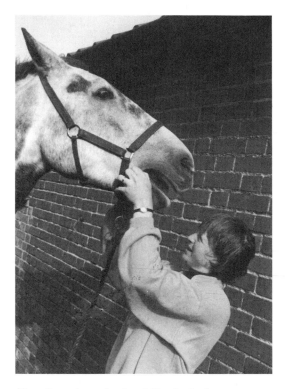

Your horse's teeth should be looked at every six months ...

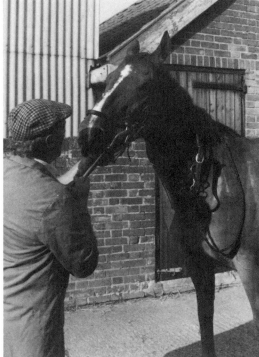

... and will probably need rasping once a year.

paddock, with few companions, or a small paddock with many others. You will need to vaccinate your horse against tetanus and equine influenza. This requires your veterinary surgeon to give your horse an initial course followed by yearly boosters for 'flu, and two or three yearly boosters for tetanus.

• Your horse's teeth should be looked at every six months and will probably need rasping once a year, although if he is over sixteen or under four years of age he may need more regular check-ups.

• If your horse is ridden he will probably need shoeing about every five or six weeks. Unshod horses living at grass usually need trimming every six to eight weeks.

Introducing a Horse to a New Paddock

If you acquire a new horse, or move your horse to another livery yard, you will have to allow him a period of acclimatization. To appreciate how he might feel, imagine that someone sold your house without you knowing. You are put in the car, taken for a journey and then dumped in another house. You will feel strange, and may even feel very angry at first. However, gradually you will come to know where everything is, and eventually claim your new home as your own. It does not happen quickly though, and there will be times when you yearn to be back in your old home.

Before turning a horse out into a new paddock, check to see if there are any hidden dangers such as chain harrows, or rollers discarded in long grass by a farmer ...

... or any litter, or large flints that could injure your horse.

Are there any poisonous plants? This is laurel, and you should know that it is poisonous to your horse.

Your horse also needs time to adjust; allow him to explore the paddock, without being made to feel threatened by any more dominant horses. He might not like to be completely on his own, however, so an old pony, or more docile horse as a companion may have a calming effect. At first he is likely to gallop around, generally getting a feel of the space. Then he will take a closer look into all the corners, and lastly he will probably sniff the boundaries and locate the water trough before settling down to graze. This may take just a few minutes, or it may take a few hours – but it will be days before he really settles.

Before you turn a horse out into any unknown paddock, you need to carry out certain field checks.

• Are there any hidden dangers such as chain harrows or rollers lying discarded in long grass by a farmer?
• Is there any litter? Broken bottles and food wrappings can often stray into paddocks, or be left by 'picnickers', particularly if the field has a right of way, so check the field thoroughly.
• Is the fencing safe and secure and are the watering facilities suitable (see Chapter 3).
• Are there any poisonous plants growing (see Chapter 5).

Don't assume that regular field checks will automatically have been carried out at a livery yard. Most places are vigilant and do carry them out regularly, but unfortunately some people just don't know any better. I bet you have seen horses grazing in fields full of ragwort, barbed wire or other such hazards at least once on your travels. Do not let one of these horses be yours.

Introducing a Horse to Other Field Companions

The other important factor to consider in the interests of your horse's safety and pleasure is that of his field companions. In Chapter 1 we discussed the horse's social behaviour and this can cause practical problems for us. Nobody wants to turn his/her horse out into a group of others only to see him kicked, bitten and generally shunned. However, unless your horse portrays a particularly dominant nature then this is what is likely to happen if you simply turn him out into a paddock with horses that are well established as a group.

Where a group of horses are all turned out at the same time into a new paddock they usually settle well after an initial inquisitive period. None of them will have yet claimed the land as their own, so each can find his own space and settle into his accepted place. It is when a new horse is introduced to an already established group that problems can occur, so introductions should be gradual. The ideal way of doing it is as follows:

1. Turn your horse out into a paddock adjacent to the one that contains the other horses. Ideally there will be a walk-way between the two paddocks, so that the horses cannot actually touch each other over the fence, although they can get used to seeing and smelling each other.
2. After a day or so, take one of the horses from the established group and turn it out with your horse.
3. After another day you can either take the rest of the group from their field and put them in with your horse, or put your horse and his companion back in with the established group.

Ideally there should be a walk-way between two paddocks, so that horses cannot actually touch each other over the fence.

There may be some initial squabbles, but this method usually causes few real disputes.

Turning a Horse Away

The term 'turning away' means letting the horse out into a paddock for a rest from work, or a 'holiday at home'. It may involve the horse living out totally, or bringing him in to be fed or stabled overnight, depending on his breeding and for what work he is kept. Every horse that has competed regularly deserves a rest at the end of the season. While competing he will have received constant attention and so needs time to wind down, both physically and mentally. If he has been showing he will have had a lot of rugs on him, so these need to be removed gradually. It is both cruel and inviting illness if at the end of the season you turn a pampered horse out straightaway to fend for himself; you must allow whatever you have taken away to establish itself once more before he will be able to cope. Only when you are sure you have hardened off your horse sufficiently well can he go out altogether, but you will still have to pick the right time, perhaps waiting until you get a nice sunny autumn day. Turning horses away also gives their feet a chance to recover from the rigours of shoeing; once the shoes are taken off the nail holes can then grow down and any little cracks will grow out.

While he is turned away it is important that the horse is still checked and fed regularly. After his holiday he should come up well conditioned and mentally refreshed, ready to start competing again.

Bringing a Horse Up

This involves the opposite sort of routine, although, a horse can be 'brought up' but still live out. 'Bringing up' is simply a term for putting the horse back into work, and traditionally this means putting him back into a stable. The right time to bring a horse up is, to a certain extent, a matter of personal choice and often depends upon individual circumstances. Some people bring their horses up at the end of December in order to get an early start with youngsters and new prospects, while others may wait until mid- to late January depending on what is planned for the year ahead. Hunters come back into work in about July. It is pointless to start work too early if you have little time to devote to riding; in such a situation it is more beneficial to wait a few weeks until you know you can commit the time required to work the horse regularly.

When initially a horse resumes work the first things to sort out are his coat and feeding programme. If his winter management and feeding regime have been well catered for, he should be in good health and carrying plenty of condition. This will ensure he stays in the best of health as work progresses.

CHAPTER 3

Paddock Hardware

The ideal field is one that has plenty of grass, natural shelter and a fresh, natural water supply. However, few paddocks meet these criteria as most horses are kept on land that is convenient, rather than naturally suitable. The more we depart from this ideal, the more equipment we will have to put into the field, in order to satisfy the horse's everyday needs. However, a field shelter seems to be one of the aspects of caring for a horse at grass that most people simply don't bother about.

Providing Shelter

Shelter is one area where I feel human intervention has improved on nature. Natural shelter is at best a densely leafed

Natural shelter is at best a densely leafed band of trees, but in pouring, driving rain the horse must still feel pretty cold and miserable.

A well-positioned field shelter, where the back takes the brunt of the prevailing wind.

band of trees, but in pouring, driving rain the horse must still feel pretty cold and miserable. A purpose-built shelter affords much more protection, warmth and comfort should he wish to take advantage of it; he can get out of draughts and keep himself completely dry.

Where to Site a Shelter

A field shelter should be erected so that the back of it takes the brunt of the prevailing wind; this is usually so that the front faces the south. It should be sited either very close to the fence-line so that a

horse cannot get behind it, or far enough away from the fence line so that there is easy access behind it. It should not be put into a corner of a field as this allows a bully horse to trap another up against it. When considering where to site it, also give some thought to the approach; for example, can you get in easily with a barrow in order to muck it out, and take in fresh supplies of hay? Try not to put it under overhanging branches as these may annoy the horse by constantly rubbing back and forth on the roof; also fallen, leaves will rot and make a mess of the roof. Although not always practicable, you

A field shelter should be sited either very close to the fence so that a horse cannot get behind it, or far enough away so as to allow easy passage behind. This shelter is sited so that it can be used for either field by simply altering the slip-rails.

should strive to satisfy as many of the following requirements as possible:

1. Try to site the shelter on the highest part of the field, as this will prevent rain from running into the bottom of it, or the floor inside from becoming too wet.

2. Try to make sure that the *back* of the shelter faces north or east.

3. Allow easy access behind or none at all.

4. Make sure the shelter is safe: no nails or other projections sticking out, no low beams or broken windows.

5. Make the entrance as high and wide as possible to encourage horses to enter, and to provide an easy escape if necessary.

6. Ensure the structure is strong enough to withstand horses rubbing or kicking the sides.

7. A single pitch roof is fine and obviously this needs to slope backwards.

Types of Shelter

There are various types of shelter that can be used. As already mentioned, trees and hedges can form the shelter to a field, but they do not offer total protection. In the winter they become leafless, providing virtually no shield against the weather, and in the summer, flies, wasps and other

A shelter suitable for a single horse.

insects gather around them and cause enormous irritation to the horse. It is all very well saying 'but that is all the horse would have in the wild': remember, the wild horse has not been groomed, so that to a great degree his natural coat oils have been removed, neither has he had most of his mane removed and his tail trimmed short in order to make him look nice. Moreover, even though these 'natural' forms of shelter are little more than useless in winter, horses still tend to gather round them; to them, a little shelter is obviously better than none. And this causes further problems as the ground around trees and hedges quickly becomes boggy;

yet the horses continue to congregate in the wet mud as they have no other choice.

When putting a man-made shelter into a field, give some thought to its purpose. Will it be used more in summer than winter (perhaps because your horse is stabled at such times); is it only required for one horse, or many more? It is true to say that any shelter is better than none, unless of course the shelter is dangerous. Where there are several horses in a field, the ideal is more than one shelter, although this can be costly and take up more room than is really available.

Shelters come in many styles. In its simplest form a shelter may be no more

A shelter suitable for more than one horse.

than a wall of straw bales supported by a wooden framework, with a waterproof covering and a roof made of corrugated iron. This can only be a temporary measure, however, and must be thoroughly secured. A large shed is preferable, and this can be bought or constructed from surplus wood. Another way to acquire a field shelter is to look in the classified advertisements section of newspapers for second-hand ones; occasionally you may see them at farm sales, for little cost. And if your stable yard butts up to the edge of the field you could utilize the end stable, making an opening in the side to allow the horses easy access.

If it is possible only to provide one shelter, then this must be large enough to accommodate all the horses in the field. It is unlikely that they will all go in at once, but it is heartbreaking to see a timid horse kept out of the shelter by a more dominant one, and to see him standing alone and forlorn in the corner of the field. If such a situation is allowed to continue the horse will surely become ill, because when he is at a low ebb mentally his physical health will be susceptible too.

An ideal type of shelter to prevent bullying.

Make sure the doorway to a field shelter it is high and wide enough to allow a horse easy access. Moreover, where two or more horses are sharing the same shelter it is preferable to have an entrance and an exit opening, so that a timid individual does not become trapped inside by a dominant one. In this respect a more sensible design would be a semi-circular or octagonal shelter; any horse which felt threatened could then easily make his escape by running round the walls to the exit. This idea does not seem to be popular, however, but should seriously be considered.

Bases and Bedding

It is not necessary to lay a concrete base for a field shelter as it is not exposed to the volume of urine that a stable is. A nice thick bed is all that is really required, for as long as the shelter is not sited so that rain will run into it, it should stay dry. When newly erected it is just as well to allow the horse to eat the grass inside for the first few days, then you can lay the bed. Do not lay a straw bed if there is still a lot of grass inside as the horse will invariably try to pick at this, churning the bed up in order to do so. In the absence of any grass underneath, other bedding materials can be used as desired.

Using a Shelter

While at first many horses will be wary of a new shelter, they will soon come to use it. Make sure it has a good thick bed inside; deep-litter beds are ideal for this job as they provide warmth and offer some protection from a wet floor underneath. As with a stable, droppings need to be picked up regularly, otherwise the horse can start to suffer with conditions such as thrush. There also needs to be a means of feeding hay in the shelter, either by using a haynet attached to a tie-ring, or a hayrack. The wooden type of cattle-racks with a catch-tray underneath are ideal as these will extend along the back of the wall at head-height, serving more than one horse at a time. They also prevent much of the waste that is seen when haynets are used.

Fencing

There are various types of fencing used to enclose horse paddocks, and some are more suitable than others. Whatever type of fencing is used it must meet certain criteria. Obviously it needs to be high enough so that the horse will not be able to jump out; equally it should not be so low that he could trap his hoof between it and the ground. It should be strong enough so he cannot push it down or snap it, and it must be clearly visible to prevent him running into it. Any sharp corners should be fenced across so there is no risk of him becoming trapped or wedged in them.

Sharp corners should be fenced across to prevent a horse from becoming trapped or wedged.

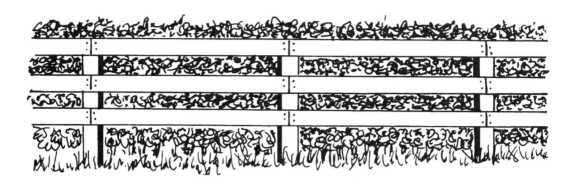

If the hedge is still establishing itself, it is a safety measure to put secure fencing in front of it.

Hedges and Ditches

Natural hedges make an excellent field boundary as long as they do not become sparse in winter and so provide a means of escape. Really stockproof hedges need to be around 5ft (1.5m) in height and 2ft (0.6m) wide at the base. They provide many advantages in that they are easy to maintain and can prevent many cuts and injuries from accidents involving fences. If the hedge is still establishing itself, it is a sensible safety measure to put secure fencing in front of it, so that the horse cannot simply push through.

A ditch is not a particularly safe way of enclosing a field. On the one hand it needs to be deep and wide enough to deter a horse from jumping over it, but on the other, a horse, if chased, could fall in and then be unable to get out.

Post and Rail Fencing

To my mind post and rail is still the best fencing for horses. It is strong, clearly visible and safe. Two or three rails can be used depending on whether ponies or larger horses are kept. To ensure stability and strength there should be no more than a 6ft (1.8m) span between posts, which themselves should be 5 × 3in

---

When thinking of planting a hedge as a long-term measure, take some advice from your local garden centre as to the best choice of hedging plants for your area. You want something that will be resilient and grow quickly. Blackthorn, holly, beech, hazel and hawthorn are often used, as they do not seem to be very palatable to the horse.

Two or three rails can be used in post-and-rail fencing depending on whether ponies or larger horses are kept. This example also has electric fencing attached to prevent sheep from escaping.

(13 × 8cm), and dug about 2ft (0.6m) into the ground. The posts should be back-filled so that in an emergency they will give, and not snap under pressure. To ensure they are protected from winter weather treat them with creosote in late summer.

Stud Rails

These can be used as an alternative to tra-ditional wooden rails. They are made of high tensile wire covered with a wide

plastic band, and are therefore clearly vis-ible and strong. They are a good choice as they need very little maintenance and are completely safe.

Wire Fencing

Whether plain or barbed, I cannot recom-mend wire for horses. While barbed wire is the most problematic, any type of wire can cause horrific injuries. When it is first put up it is taut, but it soon sags and horses have little respect for it, putting their head and legs through it at any opportunity. It is always best avoided.

Electric Fencing

Electric fencing of the sheep-netting vari-ety is not at all suitable for horses. How-ever, there is now a particularly good type of electric fence available that is manu-factured specifically for horses. It comes in wide white bands so is clearly visible, and is ideal for sectioning off fields to provide a rotation system.

Gates

Gates are usually wooden, of the five bar variety, but can also be metal. They should be sited in the centre of a fence-line, and not in a corner of the field. If horses are fed by the gate this allows the more timid to escape from others who may

As a deterrent to horses being stolen it is a sensible precaution always to ensure gates are padlocked *at both ends*. If possible site the gate where it is away from any road, or track but is in view of the stables or house.

Sheep netting attached to the lower rail can be potentially very dangerous for horses.

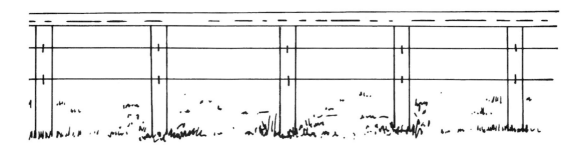

Stud rails.

Barbed wire is always to be avoided.

try to bully them at feed times, or when being brought in or turned out. It is a good idea to put down shale in front of gate entrances as this helps to prevent them from becoming boggy in winter.

Watering Facilities

Water is the most vital ingredient to your horse's health and well-being. It must be fresh and should be accommodated within a suitable, safe container. Self- filling, galvanized water troughs are ideal for horses, although they can be costly to install. An old bath tub that has had its taps removed can be safely employed; it should be panelled upwards from the bottom to prevent a horse from trapping his feet underneath, but otherwise it is quite ideal. It will need to be cleaned out regularly, but since all you need to do is 'pull the plug', this is not a problem. Obviously it does help to have this kind of trough sited near to a water supply so that refilling and cleaning can be carried out with minimal effort.

Natural water supplies are provided by streams and rivers. However, the approach must be firm and gradual, and the bottom gravelled, not sandy. The water must be running otherwise it will become stagnant. A stream that has steep or crumbling banks should be fenced off because it

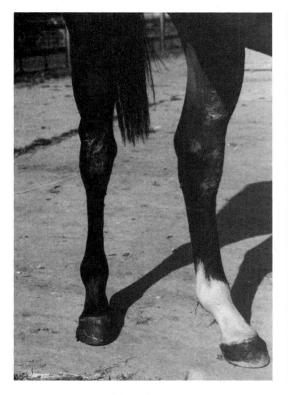

Injuries sustained by a horse tangling with barbed wire.

Water troughs should be checked twice daily during freezing weather. *This is so important that it cannot be stressed enough.* I have heard people say that their horses never seem to drink water in the winter, so they need not worry about the water trough! It would perhaps interest them to know that one of the main causes of colic in grass-kept horses in cold weather results from dehydration brought on by lack of water. If you have a horse kept out of doors you must break and remove the ice on his trough *at least twice daily.* It is your duty as an owner, and if you fail to do this it constitutes a clear case of neglect. It can help to put a heavy football into the trough as this will move in the breeze and thus prevent a small area from freezing up, so allowing some water to be obtained. A clever horse will learn to push on the ball in order to obtain water, in the same way as horses learn to use an automatic drinking bowl.

Gates should be sited in the centre of a fence-line, not in a corner of the field.

It is a good idea to put down shale in front of gate entrances as this helps to prevent them becoming boggy in winter.

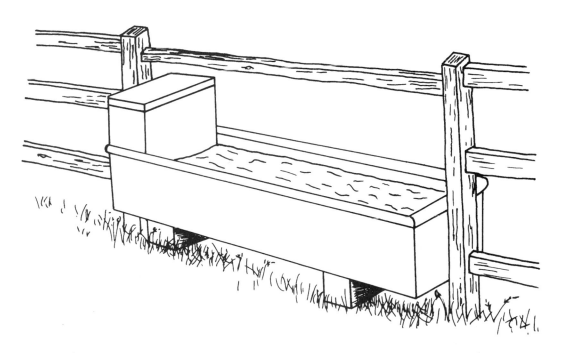

Self-filling water troughs are ideal for horses, and this one has been positioned to serve two fields.

Water must be fresh, and accommodated within a suitable, safe container.

Self-filling, galvanized water troughs are ideal for horses.

An old bath tub that has had its taps removed can be safely employed, but it should be panelled upwards from the bottom to prevent a horse from trapping his feet underneath.

An unsuitable natural water supply should be fenced off to prevent access.

A natural water supply must be running otherwise it will become stagnant.

A temporary watering facility.

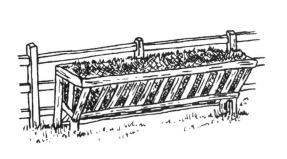

A safely constructed outdoor hayrack.

A combined hayrack and feeding manger.

constitutes a hazard; obviously an alternative supply will then need to be provided.

To help prevent water buckets from freezing inside a shelter, you should lag them. To do this, place the bucket onto a polystyrene sheet inside a thick, tough plastic bag or hessian sack, then fill the space between the bucket and this outside wrapping with hay to form an insulating layer. Tie the outer covering securely around the bucket, making sure any loose ends are tucked in. Put the whole thing inside an old tyre to prevent it from being tipped over, and then fill it up.

Field Feeding Equipment

Hay-Racks and Nets

When feeding hay in the field it can become very wasteful if you simply put it on the ground; although having said that,

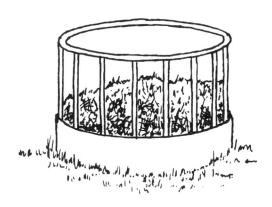

A round manger such as this is unsuitable for horses, as they can twist their heads once inside and then panic if they cannot free themselves.

Where there are only a few horses in a field, a hay-rack is a good alternative to piles on the floor.

Haynets must be tied up high, onto a tree or the side of a barn, or else the horse or pony could get a foot caught, with disastrous consequences.

where there are many horses in the same field this may be the only option as you have to provide many different piles so that each horse can eat in peace. Always provide one pile more than the number of horses, so that if an underling does get chased away from a pile there will always be another to go to.

Where there are only a few horses in a field, a hay-rack is a better alternative. These are free-standing and have a catch-tray underneath to prevent the hay from dropping on the floor and being trodden in; they can be metal or wooden. Do not use the round, cage-type of rack for horses, however, as they can get their heads stuck through the metal bars and are then likely to panic, resulting in some pretty nasty injuries.

Two types of sensible field manger, a rubber floor tub that is non-slip and non-tip, and a fence manger.

Haynets are acceptable as long as they can be tied up high enough. Often this will be to a tree or the side of a barn. Always ensure the rope cords are strong, and replace at the first sign of fraying or weakness.

Feeding Concentrates

When feeding the horse concentrates in the field you need something to put them in, and it needs to be non-slip and non-tip! Mangers that hang onto the fence are suitable, but it is my experience that horses love to pull them off and so the feed gets spilt; if the ground underneath is wet and muddy this can be very wasteful. Shallow rubber tubs seems to be the best alternative. Horses do not appear to want to kick these over, and they can be safely left in the field if you need to go off and attend to other chores.

CHAPTER 4

Practical Care

How you care for your horse at grass will depend upon where he is kept and under what conditions. Is he kept at home, or at a livery yard? Is he turned away or being ridden? And so on. Obviously you will need to develop a routine to suit yourself, but there are certain ways of doing things and certain standards that should be met.

Catching your Horse

Allowing himself to be caught by a human is something that a horse should learn correctly as a foal. It is a most important lesson and if it is not taught at this young age it can set the scene for a rather long and frustrating battle. If you have a foal that is still with its mother, be sure that you make good use of the time you have with them together: there is no better teacher than a foal's dam, so whenever you catch her up, also reward the foal for coming with her. If you do this, a foal will soon come of its own accord and will rarely pose any future problems.

Always ensure that whenever you approach your horse you do so quietly and calmly, informing him of your presence by talking to him as you get nearer to him. Always approach his head from the side to avoid startling him, because he cannot see you from behind until the last minute; it will also ensure that he cannot kick out or barge into you.

Where you have a young horse that has not been taught properly to accept being caught, you will have to employ other methods. I have found it necessary to make a three- sided pen with a slip rail to the back in one corner of the field for such youngsters, as often the only way you can catch them is to herd them into the pen and have someone slip the rail across. I must admit that when I first tried this method I was a little anxious as to how that particular youngster would react.

The penning idea can be taken one step further. At one time I had a particularly difficult horse, and each time it was was due to be fed, I put his feed in the pen. At first I did this this to a routine, and left him to eat his feed in peace. (I should say at this point that this horse was very nervous of humans due to ill-treatment in the past.) Then as time went on I would stand in the pen while he was eating. Once he accepted me, I would catch him up and just hold him while he was eating. The one last hurdle to overcome was to ensure he would come to the pen at any time, and not just at meal times. In order that he would do so, I would arrive at the pen at different times of the day with a reward for him, and sure enough he would come over. That horse has never since refused to be caught, at any time of day or in any field (with or without a pen).

Always approach your horse's head from the side to avoid startling him, because he cannot see you from behind until the last minute.

Would he panic and try to jump out? Would he turn on me? In the event, once he realized that he was 'caught' he gave up the 'game', and we only had to use the pen for him one more time. Make sure such a field pen is built with strong posts and rails, so that it will withstand a youngster pushing on it if necessary; this will also ensure it does not pose a hazard while the horses are grazing normally.

There are times when even the most obedient of horses will not be caught; perhaps having recently been turned out onto a lush pasture he would rather not come back in when you want. However, it is the older horse that refuses to be caught on a regular basis which generally causes the most problems.

Horses that Refuse to be Caught

Refusing to be caught is a disobedience. While it might be far nicer for your horse to stay out grazing, he should have learnt to respect your wishes. However, there are still a few methods you can try so as to teach him that you expect him to come when you call. What you must *not* do, (and we all feel like it at times!) is to throw the headcollar at him as he disappears down the field showing you a clean pair of heels!

The Horse on his Own
What you try will depend on whether there are other horses in the field or not. If there are not, then you can train him to come for food. At first you will need to

If he is used to being caught, slip the lead-rope round his neck so that you have hold of him before putting on the headcollar.

as well, as this encourages him to come to your voice, which can be very handy if on occasion you forget to take the reward.

Other horses can be bluffed into being caught. Should your horse not come for food, then you will have to employ other methods. If he is the sort that allows you to get quite close, then runs off when you are a few feet away, he is 'trying you out'. First put the headcollar round your neck so that your hands are free. Then walk positively down the field and continue straight past your horse. Stop when you are some way past him but do not turn round. He is sure to be looking at you by this time, but you must not look back at him: instead, walk a few paces backwards and stop again. The idea is to make your horse feel that he is not threatened but to arouse his curiosity. One out of two horses will take a few steps towards you and then hesitate. At this stage, walk forwards, away from your horse a pace or two. You will be amazed, but many horses

have a bucket with some nuts in it, which rattle quite loudly. Stand at the gate and encourage him to come by shaking the nuts and calling him. If you see him coming, take a few nuts in your hand and put the rest on the other side of the fence. If he comes to you, then offer him the nuts in your hand while you swiftly put on the headcollar. Be sure to praise him. Once on the other side of the gate, offer him the rest of the nuts. Most horses quickly learn to come if they know they will be rewarded for doing so. In time you will be able to dispense with the bucket and be able to take just a few nuts or a carrot in your hand. Always remember to call your horse

Chasing your horse around the field until he is tired out will do no more than get yourself fit, and even then you will undoubtedly tire before he does. However, you can try to harness his herd instinct. Coming up behind him will drive him on, while coming from the front will cause him to back off. Going out into the field mob handed might result in you catching your horse, but it will not teach him anything except to try harder to get away from you all the next time. He must come because he knows that is what is expected of him. Some horses will get bored if you walk after them a few times and will suddenly turn round and allow you to catch them. Always praise them for doing so, and reward them.

will take a few paces towards you themselves. Still do not look at your horse, but make out that you are looking at something on the ground. Eventually your horse's curiosity with either get the better of him, or he will lose interest. I have actually had horses who are notoriously difficult to catch almost try to stick their head in the headcollar themselves, when employing this method. Others, have unfortunately, not responded at all, and still run off at the very sight of me entering their field.

The Horse in Company

If your horse is in with a few companions you can offer one of the more obedient horses a few nuts – but whatever you do, do not take a bucket of them into the field or it is you who will be mobbed! Horses have a natural inquisitiveness, so if you ignore your horse and feed the others, you may trick him into being caught.

The most drastic solution is to take all the other horses out of the field leaving your horse alone; he is sure to want to follow them, and so will come in willingly. However, this is very time-consuming, and is simply not practical on a day-to-day basis. It would be worthwhile if it provided a learning experience, but unfortunately most horses do not learn from it and still refuse to be caught while there are other horses in the field.

Patience and Reward

In the long term you simply have to be patient. Your aim is to teach your horse that if he allows himself to be caught whenever you wish, the result is always pleasant – a treat or reward of some kind. While you are teaching him this lesson, have him in a fieldsafe headcollar with an 18in (45cm) length of breakable twine attached to it, doubled up to form a 9in (23cm) loop. As he takes the food from your hand, attach your lead-rope to the loop of twine; this means you don't have to snatch at the headcollar in order to secure him, a practice which upsets many horses. Once caught, bring your horse in and feed him. Do not ride him, or do anything that he finds unpleasant such as bathing him for instance, but make his time in the stable or yard totally enjoyable.

Punishment

Should your horse be such a difficult character that no matter what you do he still refuses to be caught, then you must punish him. The best way of doing this is to simply withhold his feed. Do not waste your time chasing him around the field, and do not relent and leave his feed out in the field for him. Sooner or later (usually after he has gone hungry for the night) he will behave himself and accept being caught without fuss. Once he learns to associate being caught with something pleasant, and refusing to be caught or misbehaving with something unpleasant, he will rarely cause you problems when trying to catch him.

Handling Procedures

When handling a horse in and around his field you must insist on obedience at all times, otherwise he will start to take advantage of you.

Turning a Horse Out

When turning your horse out, always endeavour to wear gloves because if he became startled you could receive a nasty rope burn should it pull through your

When handling a horse in and around his field you must insist on obedience at all times.

fingers. As you lead him through the gate always keep hold of it so that you can shut it quickly and so prevent others from getting out. Turn your horse's head towards you before letting him go as this will prevent you from being kicked if he suddenly decides to shoot off, giving a few bucks in high spirits.

Trouble can occur if your horse gets excited at the thought of being put back into his field; usually this manifests itself in him pulling at you, rearing on the lead' or even trying to bolt. Should your horse display such behaviour you must act swiftly before it becomes a confirmed habit. If you are on your own and are finding him hard to control, put on a lunging

cavesson and have someone else lead him from the off side as well. Use lunging reins and wear hard hats as this will ensure maximum safety for you both. Once again, what you should aim to do is to teach your horse to be correctly led. This means you should actually give him a leading lesson every day, not just when you want to turn him out. Lead him around the field, and to and from it. When leading him to his field, sometimes make him lead away from it again before letting him go.

Once you have re-established discipline and are again in control, keep 'on top of' your horse and do not let him get the better of you again. Also consider why your horse might be misbehaving in such a

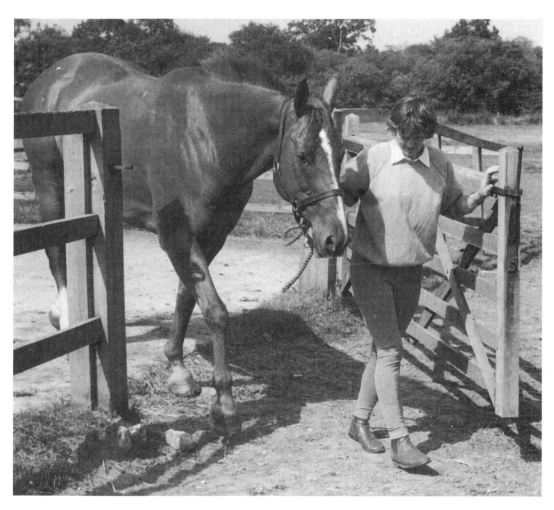

As you lead your horse through the gate, always keep hold of it so that you can shut it quickly and prevent others from getting out.

way. Do you turn other horses out before him so that when his turn comes he cannot contain himself in his eagerness to join them? If so, take preventive action and turn him out first. Also, when you do turn him out, offer him a titbit before letting him go as this will keep his interest in *you* rather than in his own desire to rush off and join his mates. More experienced help for you may be useful too.

Extracting One Horse from a Group

Getting a horse out of a field where several others are turned out too can be a problem, especially where the others also want to come in. With a single gate in the middle of the fence-line you are always in danger of letting the others out if you have no help. You are also in danger of being kicked or

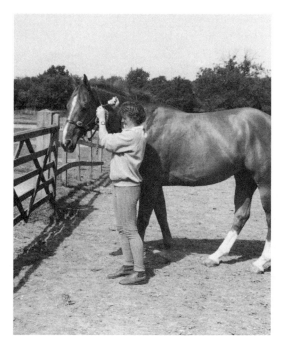

Turn your horse's head towards you before letting him go as this will prevent you from being kicked if he suddenly decides to shoot off.

A catching pen is simply a pen of about 12ft (3.6m) square with a gate on each side: one leads into the field, the other allows access to beyond the field. To take one horse in or out of the field, all you do is open the first gate, get your horse into the pen, and then close the gate. Then turn around, open the second gate and lead you horse into or away from the field, closing the second gate as you do so. This is a failsafe way of ensuring no horses can escape from the field – providing of course you always remember to close the gate you have just passed through before opening the second one!

barged if your horse feels threatened and tries to push his way out of the field in front of you. In order to make the operation far smoother, first ensure that your horse will turn swiftly on his forehand. Once you are sure of this you can take him out of the field without an assistant. Having caught him, approach the gate and unlatch it, and while holding it with your free hand, allow the horse to pass through; but keep hold of his head so that once through he has to turn round on his forehand in order to face you. The minute his hind legs are through the gate, quickly pull it shut. The whole process needs to be swift, but it is a very effective way of solving the problem, and quite easy to accomplish with an obedient horse.

You can use the same method when turning a horse out into a paddock where his companions are milling round the gate. However, if you find you cannot co-ordinate the whole movement, or your horse simply will not respond, or other horses are far too pushy, you might consider constructing a catching pen in front of the gate. This can save a lot of headaches, especially in livery yards where different horses are constantly passing in and out.

Feeding a Group of Horses in a Field

Feeding more than one horse in a field can be fraught with potential trouble if you are not quick, efficient and careful. Here are some helpful tips:
• Always have more piles of hay, or tubs of food than there are horses, so that a more dominant horse cannot prevent an underling from eating.
• Do not tip short feed directly onto the floor, but use either rubber field tubs, or mangers over the fence spaced at least 15ft (4m) apart from one another.

A catching pen will ensure loose horses cannot escape from the field while you are catching another horse.

• If there is one particularly dominant horse who makes feeding time difficult for yourself and the other horses, bring him in to feed alone.

• Try not to enter the field with feed buckets, as you could easily get kicked in the rush.

• Always remove feed tubs once emptied.

• Always ensure there is a constant supply of fresh water available.

• Horses with special diets should be fed separately, either by being shut in the shelter or stable, or by being held on a lead rope outside the field (most horses will eat their feed within twenty minutes).

Turnout of the Grass-Kept Horse

You will always have to live with the reality that a grass-kept horse will not look as sleek and shiny as a rugged and stabled horse. However, his happiness more than compensates for this fact, and he can still be kept looking fairly neat and tidy. During the summer you can groom your horse fairly well in order that he is presentable for shows, though try not to use the body brush too much as this can remove nearly all his natural oils and so make him more susceptible to chills on a cold night. Use

Do not tip short feed directly onto the floor, but use either rubber field tubs or mangers, and space them well apart.

the dandy brush as your main grooming utensil, and a stable rubber or vacuum grooming machine to remove surface dust once he is brushed. As long as the grass-kept horse is well fed and in good condition his coat should still be nice and shiny. Always remember to wash his eyes, nose and dock (with different sponges) and to dry them thoroughly to prevent small insects from being attracted to them in summer, or the wind and rain from chapping them in the winter.

Thought should also be given to your horse's natural protection. He needs all the mane and tail you can possibly leave him in order to swish flies away in summer and for warmth in winter, and he also needs his facial whiskers in order to feel things and as a protection against flies. Common sense should prevail. Yes, you can make your horse look respectable, but only clip off that which is really necessary. For instance, instead of pulling his tail why not learn how to plait it? If you need to pull his mane in order to plait it, aim to thin it rather than pull it short. In any case it is preferable simply to tidy it up by removing it at the roots underneath with an old clipper blade, or razor comb.

In the winter, grooming should be carried out carefully. Only use a dandy brush, and ensure you remove mud from the legs

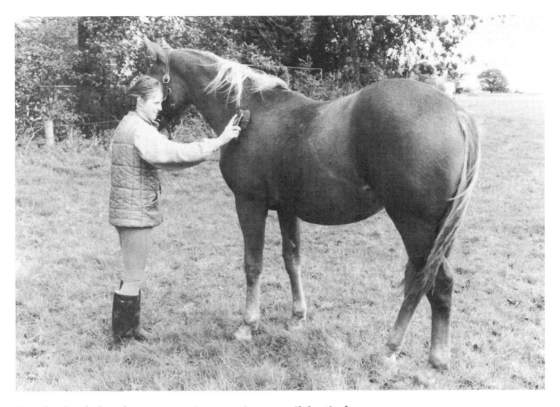

Use the dandy brush as your main grooming utensil for the horse at grass.

and heels daily. Always remove mud in order for you to ride your horse, and as you are doing so check his coat to ensure there are no signs of parasites or injuries. The tail should be trimmed so that it reaches to just below the hocks. This will prevent it from becoming clogged with mud.

Clipping

Whether you clip your horse or not, depends upon the work you intend to do with him. The best policy is to clip only as much as you need to in order to prevent him from sweating, as the more you clip the more rugs and food he will

You can bath a horse at grass, but you must be sure that the overnight temperature is going to be warm for a few days afterwards so your horse's coat has time to re- establish its natural oils, otherwise he may risk catching a chill. A good brushing after bathing will also help the oils to establish themselves more quickly. Should the weather turn unexpectedly cold or wet in the following few days after this procedure you will need to offer your horse extra protection with a waterproof paddock sheet. The mane and tail can be washed as and when required, without detriment.

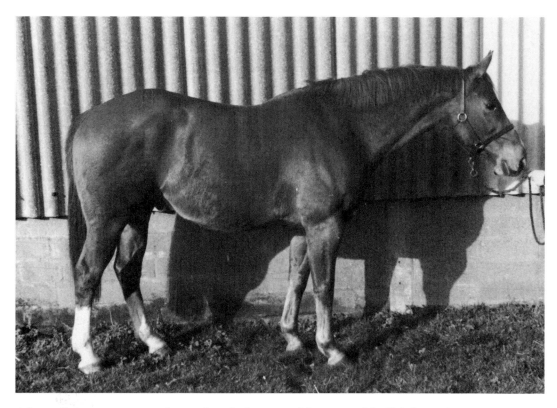

A horse living at grass can be made to look reasonably respectable (this horse is seen here in the middle of the winter) without removing too much of his natural protection.

require. If you simply go for a hack at weekends you could probably get away without clipping at all, but if you are competing and riding quite often he will need to be clipped. The horse kept completely at grass should never be given anything more than a **trace clip**, and even with only a trace clip he must be provided with a warm, waterproof rug and a suitable shelter with a nice deep bed in it.

An **Irish clip** is a less extensive alternative, as the clip line tapers off at the stifle, leaving the whole hind leg covered. This will suit a horse that is in light work only, but he will still need a good rug.

A **breast clip** is most suited to the hairy pony that is worked during the winter. It will prevent him from sweating in these areas, but will offer maximum warmth from his natural coat everywhere else.

Selecting a Suitable Rug

When it comes to rugging horses that are kept out of doors there are two schools of thought. The first is that if a horse is allowed to grow his coat naturally, and is provided with shelter and adequate food, he does not need a rug. The second is that

If you do remove all your horse's natural defences you will have to compensate for them, ending up with this!

by rugging a horse you can save both time and money, as the horse stays cleaner and warmer thus reducing the need for large amounts of food. At the end of the day it does come down to personal preference, for which mine is the latter: I am all for providing the horse with a more comfortable life and saving myself money into the bargain. However, the one stipulation is that any rug must be of good quality and fit 'perfectly'. A rug that is only just an acceptable fit is not good enough: at best it may be slightly uncomfortable; at worst it can be extremely dangerous as it may slip and bring the horse down as a result.

New Zealand and Turnout Rugs

These are the type designed to keep the horse warm and to protect him from any inclement weather. 'New Zealand' is a general term for a rug suitable for your horse to wear when permanently turned out, while a 'turnout' rug can mean a rug that is suitable for permanent wear, or one that is only intended for a stabled horse who is turned out for short periods (such a rug is correctly known as a paddock rug); so check specific usage before you buy. Most New Zealand rugs are now made of waxed

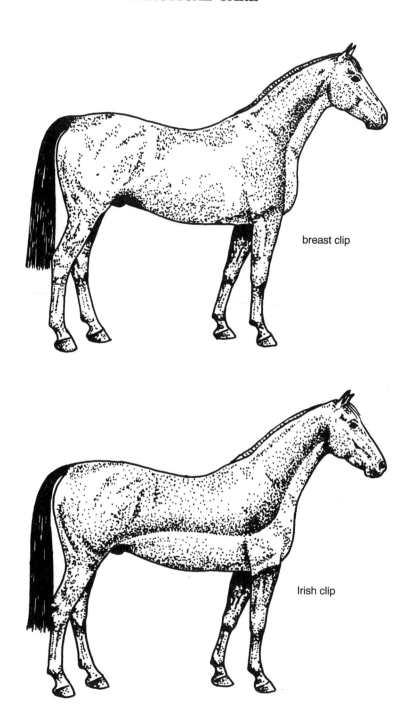

breast clip

Irish clip

Suitable types of clip for horses living out of doors (see top of next page also).

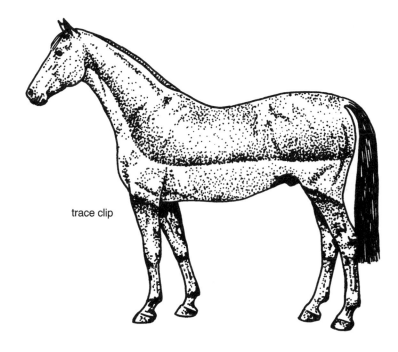

trace clip

A suitable type of clip for a horse living out of doors (see previous page also).

cotton or canvas, while turnout rugs are mostly made of synthetic materials. The depth of a New Zealand rug is all-important, for protection as well as to prevent it slipping; thus the sides of the rug should be long enough so that none of the horse's belly is visible to ensure that it is self-righting after rolling, and that it will protect the horse in all weathers.

All traditional New Zealand rugs have hind-leg straps, and some have front-leg straps as well; while some modern turnout rugs do not have any at all but are shaped over the quarters and come with a tough fillet string to keep them in place – as long as the rug is deep enough, this seems to work well, especially for horses who object to rear leg straps or have sores due to previously poorly adjusted ones.

With turnout, and New Zealand rugs, it is important to fit the hind straps so that they are not too tight, in which case they will rub when the horse moves, nor too loose so that the horse can get his hooves through them when he lies down. Link one strap through the other, and adjust them both until you can fit the width of your hand between each one and the horse's leg. Having done them up, ask someone to walk your horse on and view the straps from the rear: do they allow free, safe movement?

Rug Design

The design of a rug is all-important as some are more suitable for certain types of horse than others. When selecting a rug

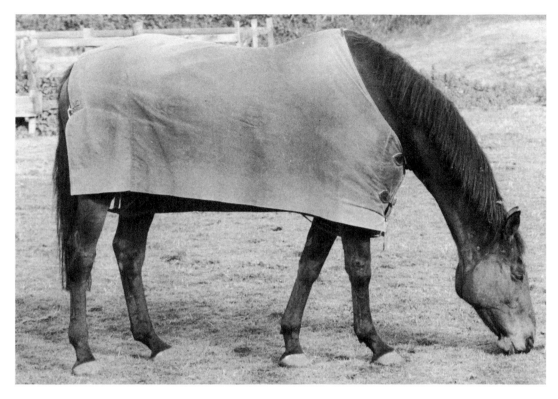

The depth of New Zealand rugs is all-important: the sides should be long enough so that none of the horse's belly is visible.

for field use, ensure that it has the following qualities:
• It should be 'horse' shaped. This may seem obvious, but it certainly is not to some manufacturers. Not so many years ago it used to seem inevitable that after a winter at grass horses would come in with shoulders that had their hair rubbed completely off. Nowadays a rug will have seams and gussets to provide a more tailored shape, especially behind the elbow, over the rump and around the neckline to offer more room for the points of the shoulders.
• It should not need a roller or surcingle. Most rugs now have either sewn-on

crossover surcingles or just hind, or hind and front leg straps. A rug that does not have crossover surcingles needs to be deep so that it is self-righting after the horse rolls.
• The straps should be easily and fully adjustable, with no lumpy buckles that may be uncomfortable for the horse when he is lying down.
• As well as being long enough from chest to tail, a rug should be long enough from wither to tail. If these proportions are not right the rug will not fit snugly.
• The rug must be deep enough: it should keep draughts away from the horse's

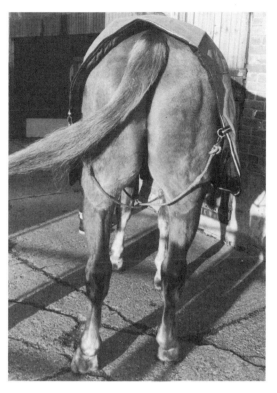

Link one hind leg strap through the other, and adjust them both until you can fit the width of your hand between each one and the horse's leg.

Some Terms that Describe Outdoor Rugs

Ripstop This indicates that the rug is made of a tough, man-made fabric which will prevent many of the small tears made by branches and the like. However, it is not a guarantee that the rug will not rip at all; barbed wire will rip anything!

Extra deep This simply means that the rug is longer on each side of the horse than an ordinary rug.

Self-righting Such a rug will fall back into place after rolling or excessive movement. It has leg straps, rather than cross surcingles, which are responsible for pulling the rug back into place.

Breathable This type of rug has a water-resistant membrane under the outer fabric of the rug which permits vapour to pass through the fabric and then evaporate. However, it will prove difficult to have a breathable rug which also has a highly water-resistant outer fabric.

---

tummy. You can buy extra deep rugs and these are a good choice for the wider type of horse. As a guide, a rug should come to *at least* just below the elbow and stifle.

The Influence of the Weather

Flies and Insects

Flies and other insects can make horses really miserable in hot weather. No matter what they do to try to rid themselves of the burden, these annoying little creatures follow them everywhere. A horse can become so irritated by flies that he will gallop around the paddock, as flies cannot keep up with a galloping horse. The problem is, the minute he stops they are back again. So the choice is either to put up with the irritation, or die of exhaustion. At least that is the choice for the horse, unless we intervene as we should. Do not count flies as simply being natural pests that the horse should learn to cope with: they are a very real threat to his health so do not underestimate them. Their bites can cause extreme irritation, to such an extent that they become sore and inflamed and even infected. To reduce the effect of flies you should:

Flies and other insects can make a horse miserable in hot weather.

The Effects of Sunshine

Sunshine is an essential ingredient to health, not only because it brings with it a 'feel-good' factor, but because together with a healthy diet it enables the horse to develop vitamin D, which is necessary for healthy bones and teeth. When the horse eats he absorbs vitamin D precursors from his food, depositing them on his skin; here they are converted to vitamin D by the sun's rays (ultraviolet light) which is then reabsorbed into the horse's body. The grass-kept horse obviously has an advantage over his stabled companion in acquiring vitamin D, unless he is rugged for most of the year. Vitamin D is included in most compound feeds and also in sun-dried hay, so the horse can obtain his source from these. However, it is far more natural for the horse to obtain it while out at grass, especially as his own body is the best provider.

• Ensure that a shelter is available, as flies do not like to follow a horse into a cool place.

• Provide your horse with a fly screen, fringe or mesh hood. A hood is very good because it does provide total protection of the head. Hoods are generally fairly large to allow for movement, but otherwise they should fit sufficiently close to the skin to prevent flies getting inside which would drive the horse mad with their frenzied buzzing as they attempted to escape from their prison.

• Use an effective fly repellent. Many of the preparations you can buy over the counter only last for a short period of time. Ask your vet about residual repellents as these can last successfully for days, rather than hours.

• Add garlic to your horse's food as this is a deterrent to flies.

(For further information, see Chapter 8.)

The Horse in Snow

Horses can do very well out in the snow without any interference from us; in fact, we can often do more harm than good by over-compensating for what *we* feel to be unacceptably cold weather. A horse's winter coat is perfectly capable of keeping him warm, and it is not uncommon to see a horse with inches of unmelted snow on his back, which just goes to prove what a good insulator his coat really is. More important than protecting the horse from cold in such conditions, is to protect him from wind.

A horse's winter coat is perfectly capable of keeping him warm even in the depths of winter with snow on the ground.

You should be vigilant, though, as the horse's feet and legs are susceptible to certain ailments in these conditions: as the snow keeps the lower legs constantly wet they are more liable to abrasions, and then of course mud fever is a real threat. In addition, you should be aware that the horse's feet were not designed for snow: they are a concave shape so the snow packs into them, forming four stilt-like shoes of ice, which can be very uncomfortable for the horse. It is therefore important to pick the feet out regularly, and applying a layer of Vaseline or grease over the foot may help to prevent the snow from collecting in them.

You should also consider the field boundaries during a period of snow. Ditches can often fill up, leaving no evidence of where they are. Similarly, ponds or lakes can freeze over, and imagine the consequences should your horse fall into either – and it does happen, as the fire brigade will tell you! So if you have these particular features in your field, be extra careful; and always have an emergency building ready to bring the horse into should the going simply become too tough.

CHAPTER 5

Grasses, Herbs and Poisonous Plants

Horses love grass, and as long as it is lush, fresh and palatable they will choose it above any other feed. The consumption of grass contributes immensely to a horse's health, indeed it is often called 'Dr Green' for this very reason. While we do not fully understand why spring grass should have such a wondrous psychological effect on horses, we do know why scientifically it is such an ideal feed source for them:

- It contains all the necessary levels of carbohydrate and protein in the right levels for body maintenance.
- It is a high-fibre source, and is excellent as such for the horse's digestion.
- It provides the body with fluid, as between 60 to 80 per cent of grass is water.
- It provides a whole host of vitamins and minerals which the body needs for tissue production and repair.

Permanent and Temporary Grassland

Grass that covers a paddock is known as 'grass sward', and a sward is made up of many individual shoots called tillers. In the United Kingdom, the season of growth starts in early spring and while initially the growth is rapid, if it is not eaten it will begin to produce flowerheads which will seed as the days begin to get longer and warmer. It is more beneficial to the sward if it is not allowed to flower, so responsible grazing, or 'topping' (cutting with a machine) if the sward cannot be grazed, is necessary for optimum grass production.

Well grazed paddocks will contain not only grasses, but clover, herbs, weeds and other various species. The main distinction between grasslands is whether they are cultivated or uncultivated. Cultivated grasslands may also be subdivided into those that are temporary or permanent.

Uncultivated grasslands are those which cover areas such as moors and dales and are generally known as rough grazing. While the forage provided might not be suitable for many finely bred horses it is ideal for native ponies and will cause far fewer ailments as a result of its comparative poverty. However, as it would be both impractical and unlikely that we should be able to turn our horses out onto such open ranges, most of our horses will be living on cultivated grasslands. Most lowland grasslands on farms support intensive dairy, beef and sheep production; the horse, however, is more likely to have access to fields that are smaller and therefore in danger of being overgrazed. Cultivated grazing may be permanent or temporary. Permanent pastures are those which are sown and then left for an indefinite period, usually of no less than

During a mild autumn the grass will continue to grow, although supplementary feeding may still be necessary as it will not be as nourishing as in early spring.

How Grass Grows

Although it may not be apparent to you, grasses are flowering plants. Instead of growing from the tips of the stems, as most plants do, they are quite unique in that they grow continuously from the bottom of the leaves. This is very beneficial to the horse, as it means the grass thrives on being eaten: the more the horse eats it, the more it grows! Although seedheads do help grass to spread from one area to another, they are not essential for the grass to grow from year to year. Grass multiplies upwards and side-ways by a process known as tillering. In response to being constantly mown down by the horse's teeth, the grass endeavours to re-establish itself as quickly as possible. Thus, grazing increases the quantity of grass that is ultimately available for nutriment. Grazing also stimulates the roots to form a strong network underneath the soil, benefit-ing the land by providing a strong surface that is resilient to horses' hooves.

Grass grows when the temperature rises above 43°F (6°C) day and night. This means that during a mild autumn the grass will continue to grow, although supplementary feeding may still be necessary as it will not be as nourishing as in early spring.

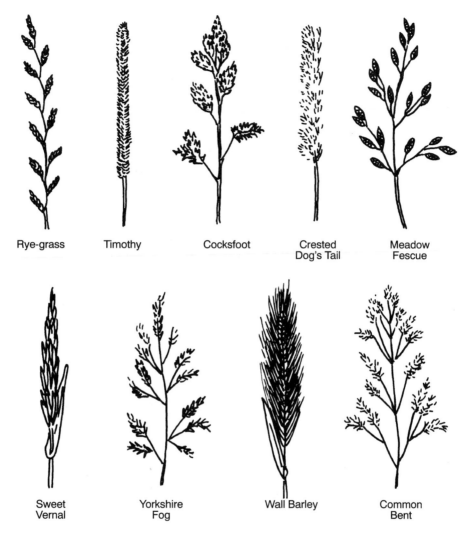

Types of grass: good grasses, top row; poor grasses, bottom row.

five years, and some may have been down for as long as you can remember. Temporary grassland is sown for a specific period and may be used as a hay crop in a rotation system, in order to build up the soil fertility and clean the land. This temporary grass is known as a ley and is normally less than five years old.

Types of Grasses Found in Pasture

The nutritional value of grazing depends upon its botanical content. High-yielding permanent pastures tend to be dominated by **perennial rye-grass**, the most commonly sown grass species in the UK, because it is very responsive to nitrogen fertilizer and is hard-wearing. It also makes good hay or silage if harvested, rather than grazed. **Clovers** and other **legumes** such as vetch and trefoil are often found in permanent grassland; they are most beneficial because they can fix atmospheric nitrogen in their root nodules, thus adding to the nitrogen supply of the sward. White clover is used in many grass-seed mixtures and certain herbs are also sometimes added. **Herb species** that are rich in minerals and palatable to horses, such as chicory, hoary plantain and yarrow, are also beneficial additions often found in old permanent pastures. Temporary grasslands are normally cut before being fed to horses, as the grasses used are not particularly well suited to grazing.

The diagrams opposite show examples of good desirable grasses for grazing, and some poor-quality grasses.

Growing for Hay

Haymaking is the oldest and most common method of conserving grass for winter feed. However, growing your own hay is a risky business. Even the most experienced of farmers can be caught out, as ultimately you are dependent on weather conditions. Problems can also result from the same factors that affect grazing, such as weed infestation and waterlogged soil. Unless your land is plentiful, has a dense, well established growth with the correct varieties of grass, it is not really worth the bother. For a start your horses may be better off grazing the land, as the money you will save in roughage and concentrate feeding may be similar to what your hay will cost you over the winter in any case. In order to grow hay you will have to ensure the grass is really well

fertilized, with the application rate strictly adhered to.

Another consideration is the type of grass you have. Old varieties are notorious for heading (producing a stalky stem with a seedhead) well before the normal harvesting time of the second or third week in June in the UK, thereby resulting in brown, straw-type hay when baled which is not that palatable. New grass varieties have been 'bred' to head much later than this harvesting date, which means they are still very leafy, with little stalk when harvested. Palatability and nutritional quality can also be enhanced by the introduction of herbs and long-stem clovers that grow in relation to the height of the grass. Such hay will provide your horse with a tasty nutritional source of roughage. So, if you can produce this type of hay, then go ahead!

Selecting Hay for Feeding

Recognizing good quality hay is almost an art in itself as it is virtually impossible to tell how good a bale is without having it analyzed in a laboratory. However, there many things you can do to cut down on the odds of buying a bad batch intended to feed your horse over the winter. First you should check that the centre of the bale is not damp or mouldy; if it is, reject it straightaway. Then consider the colour. Generally the greener it is the better, although good hay can range from green to a fawn colour. 'Sweet-smelling' is often a misleading description, as sweet hay may in fact be mowburnt: this is hay that has not been dried properly before baling, resulting in low nutritional quality. In general, hay should smell a little like fresh tea. When you shake out a section of the hay see that there is no mould, nor should it clump together. Look to see if you can recognize any of the beneficial grasses, and also any of the undesirable weeds or poisonous plants. Good varieties include meadow fescue, rye grass, crested dog's tail and timothy; poorer quality ones are Yorkshire fog, and rough-stalked meadow grass.

Basically there are two types of hay: seed or meadow. Seed hay is hard, whereas meadow hay is soft. Seed hay is grown as a commercial crop and is sown from more nutritionally valuable grasses. As it is professionally produced it is usually free from mould and weeds, although the care taken under manufacture is reflected in the price; it can be twice as expensive as meadow hay.

Meadow hay is harvested from permanent pastures which will contain a variety of grasses, herbs and possibly weeds. Although this type of hay is not as nutritionally valuable it may contain more minerals than seed hay, and it is of course cheaper so therefore more can be fed.

Feeding Silage

If your horse or pony is running with cattle he may have access to silage, a situation which often worries horse owners as they are not quite sure whether it is safe or not. Silage is safe for horses providing it has a pH (acidity) level of 5.5 or under, and as long as it is introduced gradually, so initially you may need to remove your horse from it frequently until his digestive system has had a chance to adjust. Horses have been known to acquire such a taste for silage that they will stand eating it constantly, daring any cattle to come near! In such cases you may need to tempt the horse away by putting some good quality hay in the field as well, or you will simply have to restrict his access either by physically taking him away or muzzling him for set periods.

Herbs

Many permanent, untreated pastures retain their numerous and varied grasses and herbs, but all too often landowners fail to recognize their worth and set about removing them from their horse's paddock. Species such as nettles and dandelions seem to reappear whatever you do to them, but these are not the most beneficial by any means, although horses are seen to pick at them from time to time. Given how much herbs do benefit the horse, it is not too formidable a task to set about providing them freely once again in the paddock.

Herbs are deep-rooted, slow-growing plants that contain a wide range of nutrients. Ones which may still be found in old permanent pastures include nettles, dandelion, yarrow, hawthorn, wild oat, greater celandine, eyebright, feverfew, meadowsweet, chicory, coltsfoot, cowslip, comfrey, rosehips, plantain, burdock, aconite, mint, parsley and elderflower.

Grass Cuttings

Never be tempted to offer your horse cuttings from the lawn, as a 'treat' if his paddock is rather bare. This is because grass cuttings soon begin to ferment, and this involves the production of acetic, lactic and propionic acid which in combination act to slow down the normal digestive process. As a result colic is likely to occur, especially impaction colic due to a blockage.

Species such as nettles and dandelions seem to reappear whatever you do to them.

Planting a Herb Strip

It is not necessary to plough up and completely reseed your paddock with a grass mixture that contains all the known desirable herbs; you can fairly easily set down a herb strip to one side of the field, or reseed on top of the existing sward with a mixture containing beneficial herbs. This will provide an excellent opportunity for the horse to browse on a variety of plants that are highly nutritious and medicinal, selecting those which his innate knowledge may tell him he needs. This is advantageous, as herbs generally help to keep a horse in good all-round health, and so prevent disease from taking hold in the first place.

Knowing exactly what herbs to put down is a little more difficult, as what is likely to survive and flourish does depend upon your type of soil and climate. In order to find the correct grass-to-herb ratio for your paddock, it is a good idea to contact your nearest agricultural advisory service to discover what is best for your particular situation. In the box (*see* page 86) is a brief description of the most common herbs to be found in the UK, so that you may recognize them and leave them to continue growing in peace and abundance!

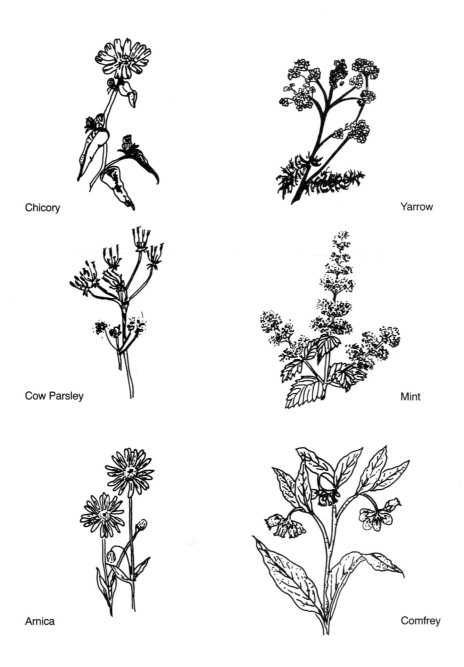

Chicory

Yarrow

Cow Parsley

Mint

Arnica

Comfrey

Beneficial herbs.

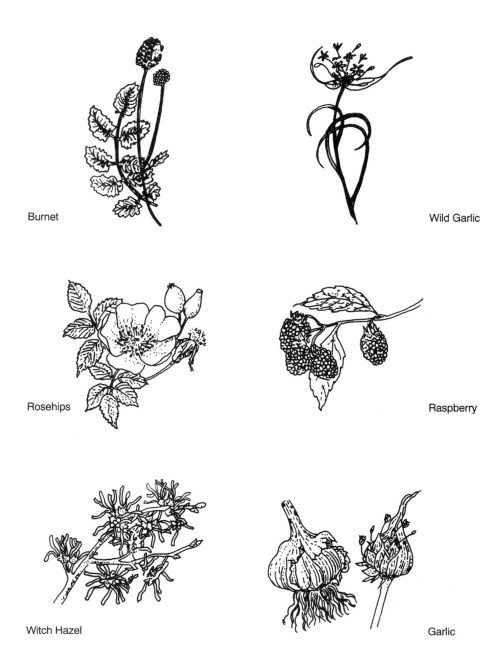

Burnet

Wild Garlic

Rosehips

Raspberry

Witch Hazel

Garlic

Beneficial herbs.

The Most Common Herbs Found in the UK

Chicory A common perennial containing organic salts, a great conditioning herb that also aids digestion. It is recognized by its rough pointed leaves and flowers that are predominantly blue, but also pink and white.

Dandelion Generally thought of as a weed due to its abundance in most fields; however, it is beneficial as a tonic as it contains vitamins B and C. It is recognized by its long roots, toothed leaves and bright yellow flowers.

Nettles Another abundant herb often thought of as a weed; however, nettles do contain a great variety of vitamins and minerals and are often used in the treatment of anaemia and rheumatism, as well as having a use as a general appetizer.

Yarrow Recognized by its mass of attractive white or pink, strong-smelling flowers commonly found in hedgerows. It is used for its astringent properties and treating bruising.

Mint A well known perennial herb often used in the kitchen; for horses it is used as an appetizer and to aid digestion.

Rosehips Characterized by their bright red, oval-shaped berries, these are found along many hedgerows. They are an excellent source of vitamin C and a valuable supply of biotin.

Comfrey One of the herbs commonly found in old permanent pastures, and has always been known as a highly nutritious healing and conditioning herb. If fed daily it provides a valuable source of calcium, potassium, iron, vitamin B12, iodine and certain amino acids. However, recently its use has been cause for debate as when taken internally it is said to be associated with liver complaints. Whether this claim is unfounded or not, it is sensible to use it with caution under qualified advice. It is recognized by its fleshy leaves and its height of about 3ft (1m).

Greater celandine Not a herb to be taken internally, but it does have a use as an external application for warts.

Garlic One of the herbs most commonly in use for horses today. Rarely will you find it growing in the field, but it is a useful feed supplement. Its use and actions are many and varied, and include the control of respiratory disorders; laminitis; fly irritation; sweet-itch; infection; worms; arthritis and rheumatism. It also helps in reducing the blood cholesterol level and blood pressure.

Poisonous Plants

We often think that horses at grass are in a safe and healthy environment, and generally they are. However, there are still dangers lurking in the form of easily accessible plants which are poisonous to the horse. Fortunately horses avoid most poisonous plants whilst they are still growing, but there is nonetheless a higher risk of your horse eating them if there is little else to eat, or if they have died and wilted. Good pasture management is essential, because as long as your horse is provided with good, clean pasture he will be less likely to eat poisonous plants. Check your horse's fields regularly for poisonous plants and if you find any, or anything you are not sure about, then dig them out, root and all.

Horses do vary in their susceptibility to the various plant poisons, depending on their condition, state of health, age, worm burden, management and feed on offer. Some horses are more resistant to plant poisons than others; unfortunately you will not know which ones are, so do not leave it to chance.

Horses will browse hedgerows so ensure you know what is contained within them.

Ragwort

Ragwort is one of the most common poisonous plants. In the early stages of growth it has a dense rosette of irregular, dark green, jagged-edged leaves, and this is the best time to remove it. From late June it grows taller, anything up to about 3ft (1m) high, with yellow, daisy-like heads. It is very poisonous to horses and causes chronic liver damage. Close grazing and low fertility of land, both of which are common where horses are intensely grazed, appear to encourage its growth.

The effects of ragwort poisoning are cumulative, so you might not notice any signs of it until weeks or months after the horse has eaten it. But if your horse begins to lose weight however much you feed him, seems lethargic or depressed, or shows regular signs of pain in his abdomen, then call your vet to check him over thoroughly.

Other Poisonous Plants

There are other poisonous plants or trees which can cause problems if they hang over into your horse's field. **Yew** and **laburnum** are extremely poisonous, and you must either fence them off so there is no possibility of your horse getting at them, or remove them altogether. One mouthful of any part of these trees is enough to kill a horse within minutes, so be extra cautious.

The **oak** tree, and its **acorns**, is another cause of trouble. If the acorns drop into

Horses will also eat raspberries and blackberries and can acquire quite a taste for them.

the paddock and the horse eats them (and some can acquire a taste for them) he can become very ill. Collecting up the acorns by hand would be an endless and totally unrealistic task, so again, fence them off, taking the spread of the branches into account. Should any stray into the field it is possible to roll them in when the ground is slightly soft. This will make it far harder for the horse to eat them, and practically impossible for him to gorge himself, which would appear to pose the greatest threat. It would seem that the problem with acorns is not so much that they are highly poisonous, but that they are very binding and can therefore cause severe constipation. Should this run to the extreme of a stoppage this could be fatal, which is why they are thought to be highly poisonous. However, as with all poisonous plants, the greatest risk comes when the acorns are the only food available.

Other poisonous plants include avocado, horsetails, bracken, hellebores, poppies, columbines, larkspur, charlock, monkshood, St John's wort, corncockle, sand wort, soapwort, chickweed, flax, alder, buckthorn, laburnum, lupins, hemlock, cowbane or water hemlock, water dropwort, hemp, buttercups, white bryony, rhododendron, sowbread, boxwood, cherry laurel, thornapple,

Ragwort is one of the most common poisonous plants.

One mouthful of yew is enough to kill a horse within minutes, so be extra cautious.

pimpernels, deadly, woody and black nightshade, henbane, foxglove, horse-radish, spotted hemlock, privet, purple milk vetch, potato, lily of the valley, darnel, black bryony, herb paris, irises, meadow saffron, aconite and fritillary.

Eradicating Poisonous Plants

The most effective way of removing poisonous plants is to dig them up, roots as well, and burn them. However, if the field is heavily infested this may leave big holes everywhere. Spot spraying is also effective, but the plant must be removed once dead, and the horse should be kept off the paddock while this is being carried out. You can top the paddock to remove the stem, leaves and head, but this must be done regularly and the debris picked up by hand, so this is in fact a much less effective and far more time-consuming method.

The Ministry of Agriculture, Fisheries and Foods (MAFF) has powers to serve clearance notices regarding certain injurious weeds on an owner or occupier of the infested land. So not only do you have a duty to ensure your horses are safe, but you must also comply with the law. This includes land outside your fences as well as inside the paddock.

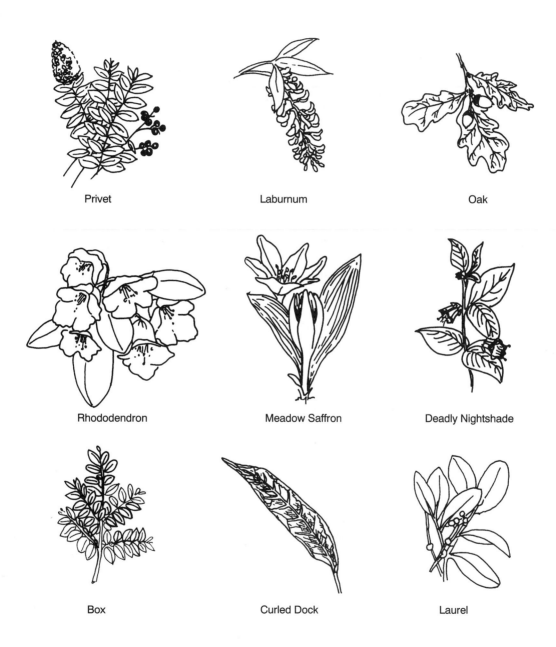

Privet

Laburnum

Oak

Rhododendron

Meadow Saffron

Deadly Nightshade

Box

Curled Dock

Laurel

Poisonous plants.

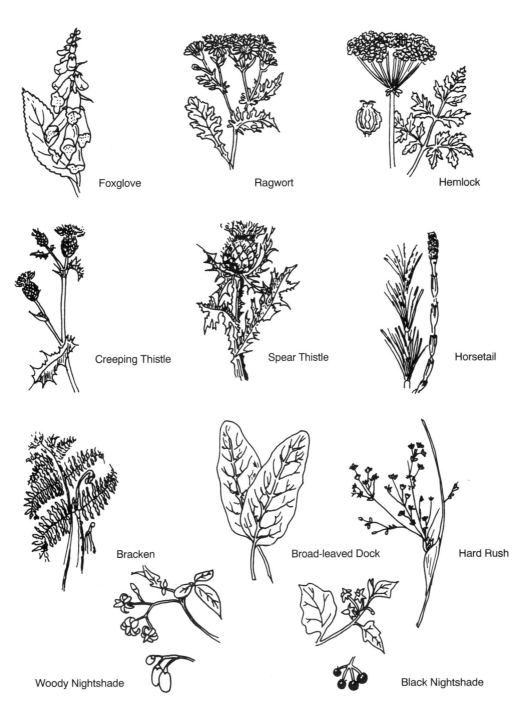

Foxglove

Ragwort

Hemlock

Creeping Thistle

Spear Thistle

Horsetail

Bracken

Broad-leaved Dock

Hard Rush

Woody Nightshade

Black Nightshade

Poisonous plants.

Rhododendrons are another poisonous plant ...

... as is the foxglove.

As with all poisonous plants, the greatest risk comes when they are the only food available!

CHAPTER 6

Paddock and Grassland Management

When we first dive into horse ownership we invariably take great care to make the right choices. Our tack has got to be of the right sort, and well fitting. Our horse has got to have exactly the right diet for his needs. We give thought to

You must ensure that your horse's paddock is large enough to provide a constant supply of grazing so that he does not have to start eating the trees, and anything else in sight!

how much the farrier's bill is going to be and how often his services are going to be required and so on. Unfortunately, one of the last concerns is often the quality of grazing our horse will have. If your horse lives mainly at grass you owe it to him to ensure that his paddock is large enough to provide a constant supply of grazing that is both succulent and nutritionally well balanced.

Keeping pasture in good condition all year round is not easy, especially where horses are concerned. We seem to be waging a constant battle against clumps of weeds, sour areas, and either rock-hard or boggy surfaces which appear within days of hot or wet weather. Unlike cows or sheep, horses are poor grazers of land. They much prefer grass that is fairly short but dense, and they will not eat grass which they have soiled in the past; these areas grow up in what are known as 'roughs', the places that are closely grazed being known as 'lawns'. Additionally, horses do poach up a paddock quickly due to their constant movement. For this reason a field that is covered by a thick carpet of dense grass will help to prevent the ground from becoming too boggy where horses are living out all the time. The absence of this coverage will result in the field becoming a quagmire, which can result in many problems, such as mud fever and cracked heels.

One of the first things you can do towards a healthier paddock is to ensure you pick up droppings on a daily basis.

Assessing the Paddock

In order to asses the condition of a paddock you need to take a really critical look at it. At first glance all may seem fine, but do you really know for sure? To establish its condition ask yourself the following questions:

1. Is the field patchy? We are not simply looking for the normal 'lawns' and 'roughs' that comprise a horse's normal grazing patterns, but areas which are very sparsely covered, where you can actually see soil underneath.

2. Does there appear to be a lot of moss and weeds, and very little else? If so your horse may not be harvesting anything of great nutritional worth.

3. Is the field poached, with many pockets of water lying about? Obviously this may only be the case at times of plentiful rain, but nevertheless it is a problem that does require solutions.

4. Does the grass generally look as though it needs some feed itself? If this is the case the soil obviously needs some sort of treatment.

Should the answer to any of these questions be yes, you need to take action to repair the damage that has already been caused, and find a way of refreshing and even improving the food source.

This amount of droppings on a paddock is too much if the worm burden is to be successfully controlled.

Maintaining a Healthy Paddock

Everyday Care

One of the first things you can do towards a healthier paddock is to ensure you pick up droppings on a daily basis. While you can get a special paddock hoover, for most of us a wheelbarrow and fork are the necessary tools. Obviously the larger the area, the less easy this task becomes. Where a paddock is very large it is probably impossible, and even unnecessary because such a paddock is in less danger of developing sour patches. In such cases

harrowing may be all that is required to distribute the dung and thus expose the worms to the elements, such as the sun's rays which will kill them.

Under- and overgrazing of land is also something that needs to be resolved. The number of horses on a piece of land is known as the stocking density. Where there is too much land, and thus too much grass for the horses to eat down successfully, the stocking density is said to be low and results in the grass growing tall and turning to seed. Tall grass is less attractive to horses, so what happens is that they leave the tall grass which gets taller, and eat the short grass

Harrowing is best done twice a year in spring and autumn, in order to aerate the soil and so enable it to refresh itself.

The ideal stocking density for horse pastures is roughly one horse per acre. However, this figure is a little confusing as one horse can barely survive on one acre, whereas five horses will do very well on five acres; this is because there will be a lot of overlap and inter-grazing within a group of horses. You can only judge by the condition of pasture, as pasture quality varies so much from area to area. If the grass in your horses' field is at the right length, is free from weeds and has a good sward or cover, then you have got it just about right.

which gets shorter. This then allows an opening for weeds such as ragwort, which thrive in deep vegetation, to proliferate the land.

Overgrazing results from a high stocking density, where there are far too many animals occupying a small piece of land. The grass is then eaten so low, that there is simply no cover at all, and this allows undesirable low-growing weeds such as creeping buttercups and speedwell to take over. It is clear then that both over- and undergrazing have a detrimental effect on the condition of the pasture and so ultimately on the horses grazing it.

Rolling a paddock is an efficient means of flattening unwanted lumps and bumps.

Harrowing

Harrowing a paddock usually involves pulling a set of chain harrows attached to the back of a tractor around the land. It is best done twice a year in spring and autumn, in order to aerate the soil and so allow it to refresh itself. The prongs on the harrows will also gather dead grass, which is detrimental to any new grass trying to get through, and they will also spread piles of dung which would otherwise prevent the horse from grazing those areas.

If you are harrowing purely to spread piles of manure, it is best to do so when it is very hot because parasitic worms which are exposed cannot survive in hot, dry conditions. Harrowing during moist, warm conditions simply gives the worms a greater compass of the field as they are carried over its entire site and the weather will not kill them.

Rolling

Rolling a paddock is an efficient means of flattening unwanted lumps and bumps. Where a field has been poached, it will dry into very hard ruts within a few days of hot weather, so the time to roll is when the soil is still soft and springy. A very heavy land roller that can be pulled behind a tractor is necessary for this job, so that the land is levelled evenly.

Fertilizing

Most paddocks need fertilizing (or top-dressing, as it is sometimes called) on a regular basis, in order to put back what the horse is constantly taking out of the soil. However, the fertility status of the the land should be known before deciding what to treat it with, as it is pointless and wasteful to provide something that is already there in abundance. Initially the pH value of the soil needs testing, because if it is not at its optimum, the fertilizer you use may not be totally effective. Acid soils are particularly troublesome because they are a haven for weeds, allowing them to take over and the grass to perish. Soil testing can be carried out by your local agricultural advisory service, and this is a good idea if you have a particularly troublesome problem. However, you can buy soil-testing kits from you local garden centre and these are simple to use and give satisfactory results.

The normal pH value for soil is 6.5, although anywhere between 6–7 is acceptable; the more acid the soil, the lower pH reading you will get. In order to rectify acidity you need to add lime to your paddocks; follow the recommendations on the bag, and reassess until you get a satisfactory pH-level reading. You will then need to reassess annually, adding lime when necessary to bring the pH level up to its optimum.

Having got the pH level right, you can start to consider what fertilizer may be appropriate. Your aim is to provide forage of good nutritional quality and palatability, and to do so you need to balance the main nutrients, such as potash, nitrogen and phosphate, with the secondary nutrients which include sulphur and magnesium, and also the trace elements – so there is a lot to cover. However, do not despair! Many manufacturers now produce specially prepared formulas which provide the correct nutrient levels in the right balance, and which are flexible enough to satisfy the needs of most pasture requirements. What you do *not* want to do is to 'force feed' the grass by using high levels of quick-acting nitrates. This will provide quick growth, but not the *quality* of growth that you want. Exactly what type of fertilizer you use will depend upon whether you want the grass for hay, or grazing. Every manufacturer's recommendations are slightly different, so be guided by the information supplied with the particular brand you use.

Dressing a field at exactly the right time can be a matter of luck as well as judgement. You want the fertilizer to go on before any new spring grass starts to come through, and within forty-eight hours of rainfall. Obviously horses must be removed from the paddocks to be treated, until the treatment has had time to take effect. This may be anything between seven and forty-two days, but certainly no sooner than the granules have been thoroughly washed in. If you have judged it wrong and no rain falls, lightly harrow the field again so that the granules are thrust to soil level, where moisture from dew will help to disperse them.

Reseeding a Paddock

If reseeding a paddock is indicated, then a good grass-seed mixture should consist of pasture perennial ryegrasses (vela, merlinda, tivoli and pippin are good examples) as this will endure a lot of grazing and general hard wear. To provide good nutritional quality, grasses such as diploid ryegrass, timothy, Kentucky Blue grass, creeping red fescue and a small amount of wild white clover should be incorporated. The addition of herbs will also be most beneficial, as these draw their nutrients from deep within the subsoil thus providing the horse with plenty of minerals. Recent grass 'breeding' programmes have resulted in new varieties of grasses which benefit any existing sward (cover), so you might consider over-seeding, rather than totally reseeding in order to introduce new varieties which will be more palatable and nutritionally beneficial.

If you have a small paddock you can sow the seed by hand, but this is a bit haphazard and of course very labour-intensive. A better method is to have it drilled professionally; the cost is not too great, and in any case the improved pasture that will result is well worth the investment.

If you have been advised to reseed your paddock completely, then you need to take a long-term view and make the very best of the opportunity while it is available to you: thus a thorough job will involve spraying, cultivating and then reseeding the whole area. Generally, grass that has been down for more than seven years will greatly benefit from this approach, but do get advice from you local agricultural advisory service, who will help you to make the best of what you have.

Reconditioning a Pasture

There is much that can be done to recondition a horse pasture without taking the drastic step of ploughing and reseeding it.

> Remember, newly planted grass has a very fragile root system, so is not suitable for grazing on for the first year. Instead of the horse cutting the grass with his teeth just above the root, he will pull it out, root as well. This leaves the soil without an underlying surface and so the ground will soon become bare and poached due to the pressure of the horses' hooves.

A horse-sick pasture will probably be overrun with weeds such as docks, thistles, poppies, buttercups, chickweed and nettles that have been allowed to spread unchecked; these need to be killed instantly, – before they go to seed – by applying weedkiller, and should be removed once dead. Spot-treatment is usually the only effective method, as many weedkillers will also destroy grass. Choose a good weedkiller that will also kill the plant's roots, and one that safely biodegrades once it has served its purpose. It can take up to two or three weeks for a weedkiller to work properly, after which time you will need to remove all dead weeds from the paddock. It goes without saying that the paddock should be rested during this period. If you simply cannot afford for the field to be empty for two or three weeks, you can use a weedkiller that will kill only the top of the plant material before biodegrading. In such cases, removal of the dead weeds can be carried out after just a few days and grazing of the paddock resumed. The drawback with this method is that the weed will grow back again, so treatment is required on a regular basis.

Drainage

Poaching of fields is very common where horses are kept; usually this is because the areas are overgrazed due to lack of space, and poorly drained. However, you can prevent overgrazing by ensuring correct pasture management; also, you need to check that any existing drainage has not become blocked by leaves and fallen debris. Moreover, you should consider the possibility of installing drainage facilities if there are none. Ideally a paddock should

Spot treatment is really the only effective method of eradicating weeds.

be on a gentle slope running down to a fenced-off ditch at the bottom, but this is not usually the case these days, as horses are simply grazed on the land that is available to their owners; this is often not very much, and not ideally placed.

Ditches are often the first option when it comes to putting in some drainage facilities, but before digging them you should ensure that there are no pipes or cables underneath your proposed excavations. Also make sure that you excavate *within* your existing boundaries, not outside them, and obviously fence the ditches off to prevent horses from falling

into them. Other drainage options include the following:

1. Field drains: these are a rather large undertaking, which will put your field out of action for weeks. Field drains entail having trenches dug, and drains installed, and then the soil is replaced. The drains are usually of perforated plastic piping with an aggregate surround, or just an aggregate channel.

2. Mole drains: as their name suggests these are created by an artificial 'mole' (a bullet-shaped cylinder) which is pulled along behind a tractor a few inches below the soil surface. These are most successful

Dead weeds should be dug up and removed from the pasture.

ly you will need to fence these off while they are establishing themselves, but in the long term they can have the added benefit of providing shelter for your horse. In certain areas it is possible to obtain grants for tree planting. It is worth checking this option; the project might not turn out to be as costly then as you thought!

Maintaining a Clean Pasture

Mixed Grazing with Sheep and/or Cattle

Rotating the land by grazing with sheep or cattle is very beneficial. First, these ruminants are much more efficient grazers than horses, as they will eat all the grass down to a level height. Second, horse worms cannot survive within their digestive systems, so they will help to clear up any worm burden that the paddock has. For most benefit, sheep or cattle should be put into the field the horses have just vacated, but it is also acceptable to graze the two together.

in clay soils as the hole remains open; sandy soils will soon start to fall in.

3. Subsoiling: this is useful where the surface immediately under the topsoil has become impacted so that water cannot drain through, and thus just lies on the top. The procedure is quite a simple one, as it merely entails a tractor pulling deep blades through the soil to break it up.

4. Trees: these are also a good form of drainage, but will only serve relatively small areas. Willow and alder will draw excess water from the land, and seem to tolerate wet land well. Obvious-

Rotational Grazing

If you have more than one paddock, they can be alternated so that each gets a rest for at least three to four weeks at a time, and preferably more. While the fields are being rested you can take the opportunity to fertilize and weed treat them as necessary. If you only have the one paddock, you can section it off in order to give each area a rest. In order to do this while keeping your horse safe, use electric fencing that is specially designed for horses (see Chapter 3).

Rotating the land by grazing with sheep or cattle is very beneficial.

In Summary

The horse has to share his pasture with various worms and parasites that are not only a nuisance but a severe health risk if not dealt with efficiently. How to embark upon an effective and regular worming programme is described in detail in Chapter 8, but in addition to this you need to put some preventive measures into force in order to create and maintain a 'clean' environment for your horse:

1. Pick up droppings on a regular basis.
2. Graze cattle or sheep on the land.
3. Rest the field from autumn through to midsummer the following year if drastic measures are needed to clear a really horse-sick pasture. This breaks the lifecycle of the worms by denying them a host for the winter.

Testing the Soil Nutrients

A scientific assessment of your soil may be beneficial if you encounter constant problems with your land. You local agricultural college, advisory service or commercial seed firm may do this for you either free of charge or for little cost.

CHAPTER 7

Nutrition and Feeding

There is no doubt that maintaining the condition of a grass-kept horse in winter is far more difficult than in summer. During the spring and summer months, an abundant supply of fresh grass is usually sufficient for most horses' needs. As the quality of the grass decreases, so the responsibility for feeding the horse properly falls onto our shoulders. However, feeding a horse in winter requires far more thought than simply offering additional food. There are two factors which govern the horse's ability to keep warm and thus maintain condition. The first are the external considerations of:

- the effectiveness of the horse's insulating layer, his subcutaneous fat;
- the thickness of his coat;
- the addition of rugs if deemed necessary;
- the provision of a draught-proof shelter;
- the prevailing weather conditions.

Then there is the major internal consideration of feed, how much he receives, of what type, and so on. The basic requirement is that he receives enough feed to maintain him, that is to keep his body functioning well. Then there are specific requirements that need to be considered which are additional to those of pure maintenance: is the horse working? Is he or she still growing? Is she pregnant or feeding a foal, for instance?

The aim therefore is to strike the correct balance between concentrate and forage levels which will supply just the right amount of digestible energy for any specific consideration, but that will also leave the horse feeling full, warm and contented. As eating uses up energy which results in increased warmth, one of the best ways to keep your horse warm in winter is to offer a constant supply of roughage, which may be in the form of hay, hayage, oat or barley straw or a mixture of both hay and straw depending on availability. Mixing hay and straw has two advantages in that it reduces the cost, and provides the horse with as much to eat as he wants. The benefit of eating for hours upon end is that the digestive system and internal heating mechanisms can work as nature intended, by constantly keeping going. Eating for sixteen hours a day is quite natural to a horse, so supplying roughage in this way is one of the best ways of keeping him naturally busy, healthy and warm.

The Digestive System

As we have seen, the horse evolved over millions of years to exist firstly on a browsing, and then a grazing diet. He had the opportunity of selecting the grasses, plants and herbs that he preferred and was able to eat for much of the day, as and when he pleased. Additionally he was able to roam vast areas, thus leaving his droppings behind and with them any potential worm hazard.

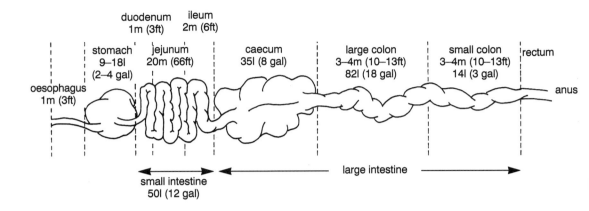

The horse's digestive system.

As a domesticated animal, the horse's environment is far removed from this uncultivated state. He is enclosed in a paddock, which in itself dramatically changes his natural lifestyle, and then we also reduce his feeding time by riding him and putting him in a stable for given periods – and to top it all, we feed him concentrates and cereals which in a natural state he would never have access to. Is it any wonder that he then becomes prone to a variety of digestive upsets? However, do not start to feel guilty just yet, as over the years horse feeding has developed into a caring art which tries to ensure that while horses are on this substitute regime, they are kept as healthy and as happy as possible.

Physical Construction of the Digestive System

The horse's digestive system consists of an open ended tube which runs from the mouth to the anus. As food passes through the digestive system it is broken down in order to release the nutrients which are then absorbed into the bloodstream. As the food is swallowed it passes down the oesophagus by a process known as *peristalsis*, where the muscles contract and relax to form waves which shunt the food further and further down with each contraction.

The food then passes into the horse's stomach, which is fairly small for his size (about the size of a rugby ball). Because of this the stomach can only cope with modest quantities at a time; if overloaded, the horse's feeding mechanisms stop functioning properly, and the food just sits and ferments. This is what eventually leads to colic, so never feed more than about half a bucketful of feed at one time.

During normal functioning the stomach empties out into the small intestine, which is where the concentrates are mainly digested and then absorbed. Roughage continues on into the large intestine and caecum where it is broken down by healthy gut bugs, which are vital to the horse as he cannot digest cellulose (the fibrous part of the forage) without them (see next section).

Once the food has been successfully processed, the waste products pass into the rectum; here, water is absorbed and dung is formed, which then passes out through the anus.

The Reasons Behind Digestive Disturbance

In today's environment the horse's digestive system has to cope with large quantities of highly processed concentrated feed, supplements and additives that are given at times to suit ourselves, rather than the horse. This onslaught is further compounded by the addition of wormers and medicines such as antibiotics, steroids and painkillers when things go wrong – a far cry from grass, grass and more grass!

Such additives can easily lead to digestive disturbances because they upset normal gut function, unless they are added gradually and only when appropriate. The horse's system cannot cope with change immediately, but it can adapt slowly. Given his natural diet of almost continuous high fibre (grass or hay), the horse's hind gut will digest the food with the aid of micro-organisms with which he produces a symbiotic relationship. These can be thought of as 'healthy' bacteria. The problem is, however, that digestive upsets can easily destroy these healthy bacteria and so the digestive system becomes even more unsettled.

Types of Feed

Grass has been the staple diet for the horse since it evolved and while through-

Digestive upsets have obvious consequences in the short term such as colic or diarrhoea, but what of long-term effects? Should we be looking to avoid having to use drugs and digestive-upsetting treatments altogether by putting less demands on our horses in the first place? Is there a way of adjusting our horse's diet to enable him to cope better with changing conditions and modern drugs? This is something that is currently being looked into, but whatever the outcome, one thing is for sure: problems only arise when humans interfere, so it is up to us to help our horse to eat his way to health.

out the year it may vary in its nutritional quality it does provide a balanced diet. Having said that, things then become more complicated if you want to work or breed from your horse. In the winter, grass will not usually have a high enough feed value for him and so it will need

I would like to stress the importance of *grass* as a feed source. As a very knowledgeable horse lady once put it quite clearly:

'You wouldn't go out and buy a puppy without receiving a diet sheet from the breeder, but it is perfectly possible to buy a horse without having the first idea of what to feed it. The new owner then sees that everyone else in the yard is feeding their horse concentrated feed, so he or she does the same. It is a great shame that more people are simply not aware that the horse does very well on his natural diet of grass. He will have far fewer health problems as a result and in return the owner will find he has a much more amenable creature on his hands.'

supplementing with concentrates or more highly nutritious forage.

I am often quite wary of telling people to increase their horse's nutrients, but if you read these pages you will realize that it is not a haphazard business, but something that needs careful thought and constant assessment. Basically, when the horse goes into winter, if he is being worked or is carrying or feeding a foal then his or her requirement for nutrients (energy, protein, vitamins and minerals) increases. In order to satisfy this added requirement we feed the horse grain-based feeds, but we must always remember that these would not ever have been naturally available to the wild horse, so his system has not evolved to cope with them; therefore some degree of caution must be exercised.

Conventionally we have always offered 'straight' feeds such as oats, barley, bran and flaked maize. However, we now know that some of the more important nutrients are deficient in such feeds and so they do not exactly satisfy the horse's requirements. The two courses available to us then, are either to balance the straights with added nutrients in order to rectify the situation, or to feed specially prepared nuts or mixes (compound feeds) that have already been scientifically balanced by equine nutritionists. Reputable feed companies take most of the 'guesswork' out of feeding horses and I have yet to find a horse that is not happy on one or other of these compound feeds.

Wherever possible all my horses are kept at grass for as much of the year as their breed allows. When considering their concentrate feed however, I am not a traditionalist. Thus, if I have a horse in hard work I choose a compound mix that has been formulated for the hard-working horse; if I have a brood mare in foal I choose a breeding mix, and so on. Should I encounter any problems, I telephone the feed company, ask to speak to their nutritionist and usually have the solution within a few minutes. When we appreciate that *whatever* we feed as a short feed is unnatural to the horse, it is easier to comprehend that feeding horses is a science; so unless you are well qualified in the field, why not take advantage of the knowledge of others? These feeds really are the answer for the average horse owner who lacks the knowledge to be able to balance 'straights' correctly, or who like me simply wants an easy life both for myself and my horses. When considering the advantages of compound feeds, also bear in mind that a single bag of mix or nuts is used up far more quickly that four single bags of straight feeds. This means that every bag of compound feed you give will still retain its nutritional values, while the straights will be losing theirs and may even be stale by the time you come to the end of each bag.

Nutrient Requirements

By the beginning of autumn nearly all the nutritional goodness will have gone from grass, but nevertheless it is still a good source of roughage, and as long as the horse consumes enough of it, his digestive system will be kept in good order. But although at around this time of year horses and ponies may *look* well with large bellies, this is deceptive and is in fact due to the intake of large quantities of poor quality grass or hay rather than any real weight being gained. Should this be the case you need to upgrade the nutritional value of your horse's roughage. You can do this either by changing to alfalfa as a hay/grass replacer, or by feeding grass cubes mixed with chaff. If the ground is dry it is often better to scatter this mixture around the paddock as this will prevent the horse from eating it in one go and will encourage him to search and thus 'work' for his food, keeping him occupied for quite some time.

Such a feeding regime is likely to be quite sufficient to maintain a horse that is not working; however, one that is having just a short holiday needs to be kept in good enough condition so he finds it easy to come back into work, without there being any necessity to build him up first. Good quality hay will provide all the nutrients he requires, but sadly such hay is often in short supply and it may therefore be necessary to add some concentrates just to keep him ticking over. These concentrates may consist of horse and pony cubes, a coarse mix or alfalfa nuts, mixed with chaff. Sugar beet is an ideal additive as it provides high levels of digestible fibre; and try ultra beet, a specially prepared sugar-beet feed that does not need soaking before feeding. This can be extremely useful and convenient in freezing weather where you cannot get water easily, or where the sugar beet itself freezes when soaked.

It is perfectly possible to work and compete with a horse that is kept out of doors. The horse will need as much, if not more feed than his stabled companion in order to keep warm, but there are various things you can also do to help him retain body heat, as described at the beginning of this chapter. The working horse must be fed at least twice a day, though often he will require a level of concentrates that exceeds a maximum overall feed weight

A good alternative to concentrate feed for non-working grass-kept horses is a feed block. These are an excellent idea as they provide all the essential energy, protein, vitamins and minerals that the horse may need, with the added benefit that he can help himself as and when he likes.

of 9lb (4kg); since 4½lb (2kg) is the maximum the stomach and digestive system can cope with at one time, the solution must be to feed him more regularly, and four times a day is not that uncommon.

Vitamins and Minerals

The right balance of vitamins and minerals of the appropriate type are essential to the health of the horse and are necessary for optimum functioning, from correct hoof growth to energy production, in order to keep a horse content and healthy in the midst of winter. Few grass-kept horses are deficient in either vitamins or minerals unless they are obliged to graze poor quality, over-horsed pasture. Should you suspect a deficiency you can select an appropriate supplement from a reliable company and it will provide all the necessary major vitamins, minerals and trace elements. However, it is sensible to have your vet check your horse's levels first as supplements are only based on average analyses of pasture and forage; if your individual horse has a specific need he may need additional quantities of one or more of these.

Proteins

Proteins are very complex substances that are made up of chains of blocks called amino acids. There are about twenty of these amino acids which can be arranged in literally hundreds of formulations, resulting in a huge variety of structures as distinct as meat and hair. The horse's body is capable of producing ten of these amino acids, but the others (known as essential amino acids) must be acquired from a different source, this being food. It is therefore essential that we feed what are known as 'good quality' proteins, which are those containing the missing amino acids that the horse's body requires. Should only one of these amino acids be missing, then the horse's diet will become unbalanced which in turn limits the use of the other amino acids that are present; this is when a protein deficiency occurs. Generally a horse on a maintenance regime or in light work only and kept on good pasture will receive all that he needs from the grazing. However, a good variety of essential amino acids may be needed for specific situations, including:

- performance horses;
- horses that have a very demanding schedule;
- breeding stock;
- horses in poor condition;
- horses that have just finished an arduous season and are in 'light' condition.

Carbohydrates

Carbohydrates are sugars and starches that the horse converts into *glucose* and *glycogen*, the substance which provides energy to fuel the muscles. Generally the less work the horse does, the less need he has for high levels of carbohydrate as fat can be used for energy when necessary. As well as providing energy, carbohydrates also help to clear toxins from the body: they help in development and also in keeping the heart contracting strongly and regularly.

Fats

Fats can be used for high energy production. They are necessary for healthy blood vessels, muscle cells and nerve sheaths. Unsaturated fats are better than saturated ones, and are a good source of vitamin E.

Supplements

Supplements are only required if the horse is deficient in certain minerals and vitamins (which is uncommon for horses at grass) or if you are feeding unbalanced

---

Probiotics

Probiotics are live microbial feed supplements that help to re-establish healthy gut bacteria that have been destroyed, perhaps due to stress or medical treatment. As they can be fed orally, they are an excellent and quick way of putting back what has been taken out, especially as this would take considerable time if nature were left to run its course. The benefit is that the horse will return speedily to his normal healthy state, whereas normally he would deteriorate before recovering. Traditionally probiotics are used only in times of stress, but some people feed them on a regular basis in order to make food more digestible and thus help the horse to gain condition. However, this is rarely justified for the average horse living at grass.

'straights'. For the average horse that is expected to do no more than most riding club work, completely balanced cubes or mixes are ideal and will provide all the nutrition the horse needs. If you start to add straights such as oats or bran to the diet, you are actually unbalancing it, and so supplementation may be desirable. I am of the opinion that it is pointless to try and mix your own feeds when today there are some excellent mixes and cubes that have been formulated by specialist equine nutritionists. Why make your job even harder than it already is?

Feeding Herbs in Short Feed

Herbs can be grown and fed fresh in short feed, but this is often impractical so most owners choose the easier option of feeding dried herbs. There are many herbal supplements on the market which make life a whole lot easier, as a couple of measures of dried herbs may amount to many pounds of fresh plants. However, the use of herbs needs a common-sense approach; it is pointless adding to the feed something in which the horse is not deficient simply because you feel it will do him some good. Nevertheless there are many general herbal supplements used as tonics and conditioners, and on the whole these are fine. As with adding a little oil to the feed, they help with health and vitality, really 'bringing out the shine'.

Feeding herbs is beneficial because they contain a vast quantity of available nutrients and chemicals in a naturally balanced form. However, if you are trying to treat a particular problem then it is best to take advice from a specialist before proceeding. For instance, before trying to rebalance a deficiency, you must know exactly what it is your horse is deficient in. You cannot make assumptions: simply because your horse's feet are crumbling you should not assume he has a biotin deficiency; it is just as likely that he has a clinical condition which needs veterinary treatment.

Practical Ration Formulation

It is well known that a horse's nutritional requirements increase with cold weather, although a high wind-chill factor will be more draining than a still cold day. In order to keep a check on your horse's weight you need to get a base value at the commencement of the winter. If your horse is a good weight, then your job is to try and maintain him at this weight; if he is a little on the lean side he will need building up, and he will need to be slimmed down if rather fat. The first step in working out how much to feed, is to determine your horse's bodyweight and the best way of doing this is to use a weighbridge, remembering to take your own weight into account when holding him. If you cannot gain access to a weighbridge you can use a special weigh-tape for horses. You will need to take a measurement of the *heart girth*, which is taken around the horse just behind the withers, and a measurement of his *length* from the point of buttocks to the point of shoulder; then put these two measurements into the following equation to find out your horse's bodyweight:

Bodyweight (lb) = heart girth (inches)^2 × length (inches) ÷ 241.3

or kilograms:

Bodyweight (kg) = heart girth (cm)^2 × length (cm) ÷ 8717

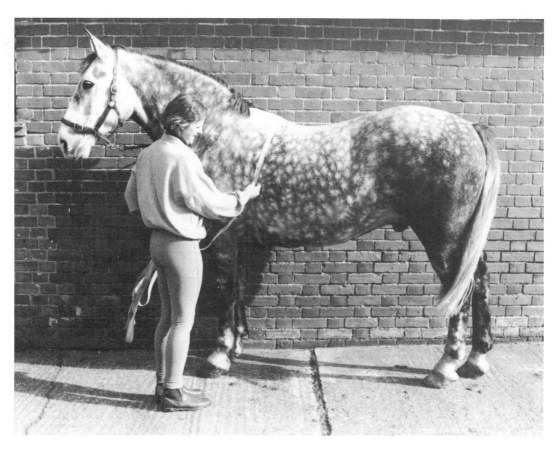

The first step in working out how much to feed, is to determine your horse's body weight. First by measuring the heart girth ...

Having worked out your horse's weight, you can then begin to devise a ration for him in accordance with the work he is doing. The average horse should receive about 2.5 per cent of his bodyweight in feed per day, and inevitably you will find yourself continually assessing your horse's condition and his diet accordingly.

Your horse's appearance is the best indication of whether you are success-fully providing him with a good, balanced feeding programme. Be guided by his condition, and once you have found a routine that works, don't be tempted to fiddle around with it. At least once a month you should make a point of assessing his condition by measuring him, because when you see your horse day in, day out, small changes may be occurring which you might not notice.

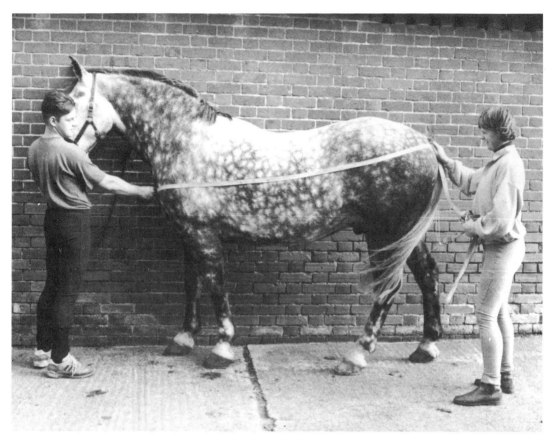

... and then his length.

There are special considerations to bear in mind when feeding the grass-kept horse:
• A fat horse is not a healthy horse, as his heart and joints will be under stress. However, when going into the winter it is preferable for your horse to be little over-weight rather than under-weight.
• As long as he is being reasonably fed, a 'good doer' always seems to keep condition on whatever his workload, and this type of horse often thrives out of doors.
• Horses with less-than-perfect conformation are often more difficult to keep in good condition, so you may need to use more rugs, and to feed more if this type starts to deteriorate.
• You need to be careful when feeding young horses. While they need enough food to maintain healthy growth, they must not become too fat as this would put unnecessary strain on their growing joints.

A horse in 'ideal' condition.

A horse in fat condition.

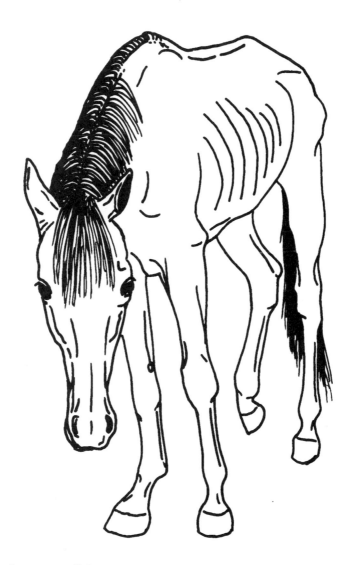

A horse in extremely poor condition.

Condition Scoring

In order to assess condition, stand directly behind your horse in order to evaluate how much flesh is covering his pelvis, quarters and flanks. Also check your horse's ribs, backbone and neck. Look at them and feel them to ascertain whether he is generally fat, thin or about right. Using the illustration on page 114, match up how your horse looks and feels with the appropriate diagram

Back   Pelvis

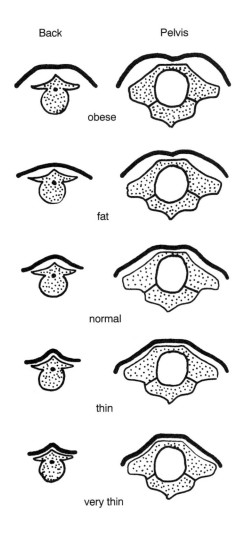

obese

fat

normal

thin

very thin

In order to assess condition, stand directly behind your horse in order to evaluate how much flesh is covering his pelvis, quarters and flanks.

Condition scoring.

to get an idea of his condition. Record the date when you do this, and if you continue to carry out a condition assessment at regular intervals, you will soon see if your horse is being maintained at his optimum weight, or is gaining or losing weight. This will help to provide a valuable guide to his feeding and work

Should your horse be losing weight without any apparent cause you should involve your vet, who will find your horse's condition profile extremely useful. Weight gain can usually be controlled yourself by limiting your horse's grazing or exercising him more. Gross obesity is dangerous to health, so again involve your vet before working a very fat horse, and introduce any exercise programme gradually.

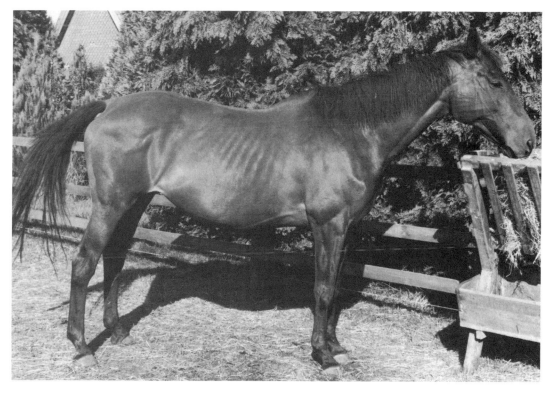

Should your horse be losing weight without any apparent cause you should involve your vet, who will find your horse's condition profile extremely useful.

programmes. When recording your condition score at each interval, also make a note of the work your horse is doing and the feed he is receiving. You will find that this proves to be a valuable guide in times of illness or extra workload, when you can quickly establish what is normal for your horse. While your horse is maintaining a normal condition, do not alter his feed unless his workload demands it. If your horse is nearing obesity, you must reduce his feed and similarly, a horse that is thin will obviously need his feed increased.

CHAPTER 8

Internal and External Parasites

Worms and Worming

Worms are an inevitable problem of horse ownership. Every horse has them, but he can do nothing about them himself as long as he is kept in small paddocks. When he lived in the wild, worms would not have been a problem because he would not have been grazing the land so intensively and so would not have taken these parasites back into his body. Worming is an area of horse management that falls completely on our shoulders. If we neglect it, we might just as well get our money and throw it down the drain, because what you put into the horse will be helping to feed the family inside him, instead of benefiting *him*.

The Importance of a Worming Plan

If you do not ensure your horse is wormed regularly he may become very ill indeed. In the early stages he will simply start to lose condition, feel lethargic and generally not be able to perform as well as he might. If this situation is left unchecked, he may develop diarrhoea and suffer from repeated bouts of colic. And if still allowed to continue, a heavy worm burden can result in permanent damage to the horse's intestinal system, besides which worms can burrow their way through the gut wall and travel in the bloodstream to the

liver, lungs and heart – so death can be the ultimate result.

Worms present an all-year-round problem for owners. There are various types which are more troublesome at various times of the year, but generally the horse needs to be wormed on a regular basis in order to catch all types of worms at all stages in their development. Thus a correct worming programme not only benefits the

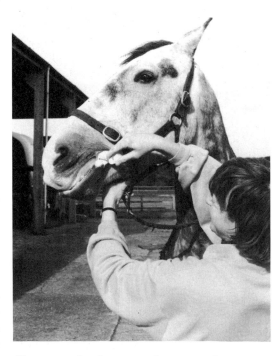

Horses need to be wormed on a regular basis in order to catch all types of worms at all stages in their development.

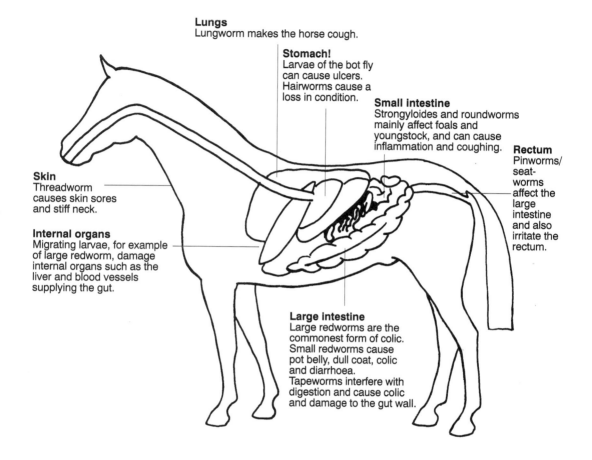

Lungs
Lungworm makes the horse cough.

Stomach!
Larvae of the bot fly
can cause ulcers.
Hairworms cause a
loss in condition.

Small intestine
Strongyloides and roundworms
mainly affect foals and
youngstock, and can cause
inflammation and coughing.

Rectum
Pinworms/
seat-
worms
affect the
large
intestine
and also
irritate the
rectum.

Skin
Threadworm
causes skin sores
and stiff neck.

Internal organs
Migrating larvae, for example
of large redworm, damage
internal organs such as the
liver and blood vessels
supplying the gut.

Large intestine
Large redworms are the
commonest form of colic.
Small redworms cause
pot belly, dull coat, colic
and diarrhoea.
Tapeworms interfere with
digestion and cause colic
and damage to the gut wall.

Sites of worm damage.

horse directly, it also reduces the worm burden on the land.

As a general rule all horses need worming at six- to eight-weekly intervals. However, any worming programme is only effective as long as all horses are included in it. In a livery yard situation all owners must get together to worm their horses all at once, otherwise your single worming programme will be a waste of effort as other horses will re-infect your horse. There are benefits to maintaining a worming programme in a yard situation: you can usually buy in bulk, so the wormers are cheaper; and there are more hands to pick up the droppings regularly.

Administering Wormers

Wormers come in granules, oral paste and injection form, so there is really no excuse for not getting them into the horse in one form or another! However, it is not quite as simple as that, as firstly you need to work out how much to give your horse. The correct quantity of wormer is related to his size: the bigger he is, the more wormer he will need. Either use a weigh-bridge or a weigh-tape to get an accurate assessment of his weight. Then dose with the correct type of wormer for the time of year, at the correct dosage. Some treatments are designed to be more effective at certain times of the year, so make sure you are using an appropriate one:

• to kill bots you will need to use the appropriate wormer in late autumn;
• to kill tapeworms double-dose your horse with the appropriate wormer in late autumn and again in mid summer.

Worms and their Life-Cycle

There are many different strains of worms which can be troublesome to horses of different ages. For instance, foals are very susceptible to large roundworms and threadworms, whereas redworms are a risk to horses of all ages. Generally the main worms to worry about are round-worms, redworms, pinworms, tapeworms, lungworms and the larvae of bots.

The **redworm** is the most common worm originating from the Strongylus species, accounting for about 90 per cent of the horse's worm burden throughout the year. The group comprises large redworms of ½ to 2in (1.5 to 4.5cm) long, and small redworms of between ⅜ to ½in (1 to 1.5cm). The small redworms can be particularly

problematic as they hibernate into the gut wall (known as *encysted* worms at this time) during the autumn, and so may not be totally controlled by worming drugs. Huge numbers can survive, causing awful damage to the gut wall when they emerge in the early spring. During their normal life-cycle, once the larvae of the large red-worm are inside the horse they migrate through the intestinal wall, then into the bloodstream where they can cause blood clotting and blockage of the blood vessels to parts of the bowel. The mature adults will return to the intestine to lay their eggs, and in the process damage the bowel lining. Once eggs are passed out in the fae-ces of infested horses, they hatch out into larvae which migrate to the grass, and are then eaten by the same or another horse; and so the cycle, which takes seven months to complete, starts all over again.

Regular preventive treatment is neces-sary for these worms. Preparations con-taining ivermectins and oxfendazole are effective against both adult worms and larvae, and the dose is usually adminis-tered every six weeks. There is at present a new type of wormer that is administered in the early winter months which is meant to destroy these worms at this stage in their development, so rendering them harmless; ask your vet for further details.

Roundworm (*Parascaris equorum*) is a member of a species known as 'ascarids', growing up to 12in (30cm) long, they are the largest of the equine roundworms. The eggs of the roundworm hatch out into the intestine, and the resulting larvae then migrate through the bloodstream to the liver and lungs. Their fate is then either to be coughed up by the horse or to travel up the horse's windpipe them-selves, where once seated at the rear of the mouth they are then swallowed again,

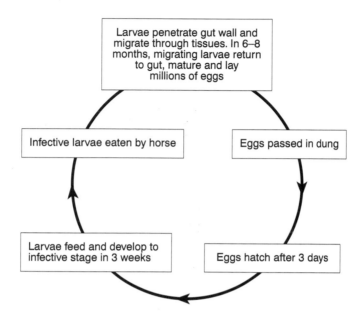

Life cycle of the large redworm.

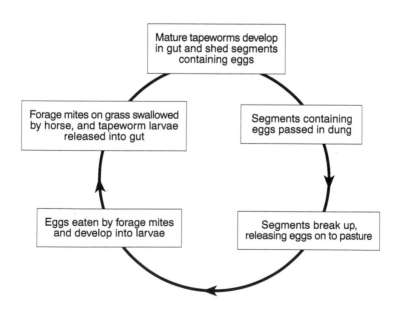

Life cycle of the large tapeworm.

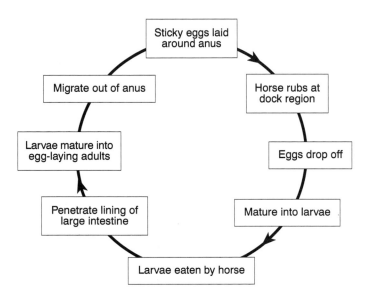

Life cycle of pinworm, four to five months.

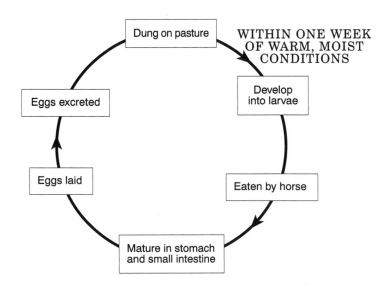

Life cycle of stomach hairworm.

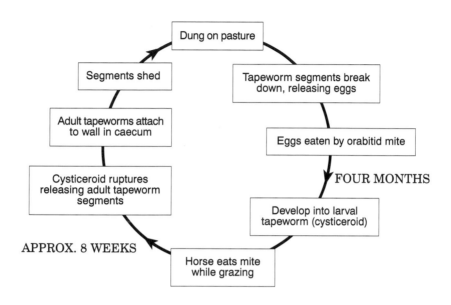

Life cycle of tapeworm, approximately six months.

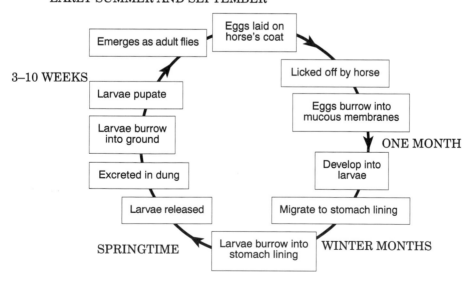

Life cycle of bot, ten to thirteen months.

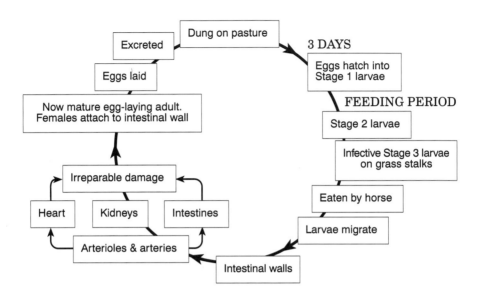

Life cycle of large strongyle, six to twelve months.

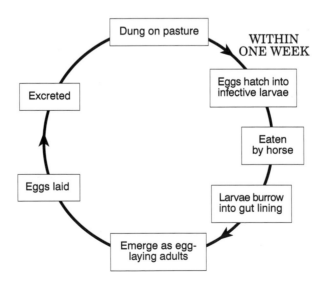

Life cycle of small strongyle, six to twelve weeks.

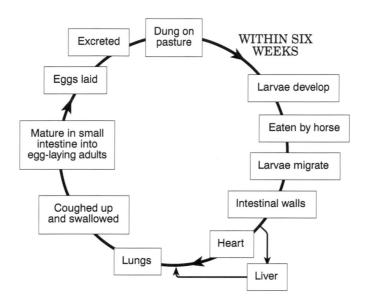

Life cycle of roundworm, ten to twelve weeks.

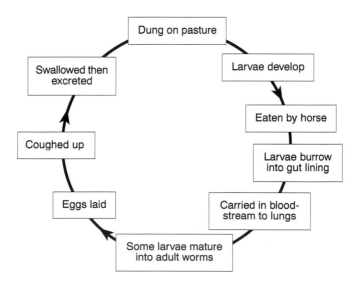

Life cycle of lungworm, approximately six weeks.

horse's feed. The adult tapeworms shed the segments of their bodies which contain eggs, and these are passed out onto the pasture in the droppings. The eggs are released and eaten by small mites which live at the base of the grass; these mites are then eaten by the horse during grazing. Twice-yearly dosing with a double dose of Strongid-P (Pyrantel) in spring and autumn helps to keep them under control.

Bot fly eggs are deposited onto the horse's hair, usually around his legs and chest, and can be distinguished as clumps of yellow specks in late summer. The hatching of the eggs distributes an itchy substance onto the horse's skin which encourages him to lick at it and thus take the larvae into his mouth. They eventually find their way into the horse's stomach where they pupate and grow, becoming up to 1in (2.5cm) long. The mature larvae are then passed out in the faeces, where the adult flies hatch and fly away, ready to lay eggs on another horse, perhaps even the same one. Eggs can be removed by grooming and scraping off, thus initially reducing the number taken in by the horse. Once all the adult flies have been killed off by a frost, a wormer such as ivermectin or an organophosphate-based preparation should be given to the horse. Were every horse to be dosed in this way, bot flies would be completely eradicated.

Threadworms (*Strongyloides westeri*) are a constant threat to foals as they can enter through the dam's milk. They can also enter directly through the skin, and usually cause scouring.

Lungworms (*Dictyocaulus*) are worms that normally only affect donkeys. However, where horses are grazed with donkeys they can cause an irritation of the airways, resulting in a hacking cough.

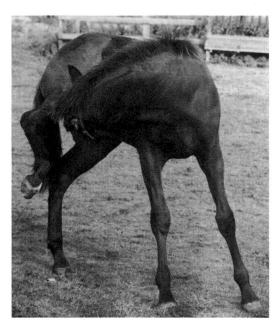

If your horse seems to be annoyed by his rear end, investigate further as pinworms may be the cause.

returning to the intestine ready to lay their eggs and restart their cycle. The anthelmintic citrazine, and also ivermectins given orally are effective against both adult and larval forms.

Pinworms (*oxyrus equi*) – or *seat worms* as they are also known – live near the horse's anus. Should you notice your horse starting to rub his tail or generally seem annoyed with his rear end, investigate further because pinworms may be the cause. This rubbing results from the sensation of the adult female who pushes her tail out of the anus in order to lay her eggs on the perineum. All modern wormers are effective against pinworms.

Tapeworms (*Anoplocephala peroliata*) attach themselves to the wall of the gut, and there endeavour to absorb some of the

Lungworm can be a threat where horses or ponies are grazed with donkeys.

Flies

There are many types of fly that are troublesome to horses. *Musca domestica* (**house flies**) are those which are attracted by fluids, so they collect around the nose, the eyes and the vulva, and any areas of broken skin. They cause immense irritation around the eyes as they are particularly attracted to tears; the unfortunate result of their activity is excess tear production which then exacerbates the problem – more tears, more flies! – because it is in these moist areas that flies lay their eggs. The larvae can then cause tissue damage, and this may result in a secondary bacterial infection known as 'fly-strike', wounds can become fly-bound in the same way if not treated promptly with insecticidal wound powders or creams. Incidentally, the type of flies that

irritate the horse's ears are known as **similium flies** and are a different type altogether.

Stomoxys calcitrans is commonly known as the **stable fly** although this does not mean it will only affect stabled horses! Their bites are particularly nasty because as they suck the horse's blood their saliva can cause an allergic reaction resulting in painful swellings.

Tabanus, or the **horse fly** as it is more commonly known, gives a particularly deep bite which is very painful to both horses and humans. Horses are acutely aware of when one is trying to attack them, and they will gallop around in order to get away from it. These flies accomplish their bite by using their knife-like mouthpieces literally to slash the skin in order to create a pool of blood on which to feed. Apart from the pain of the bite they do pose a threat

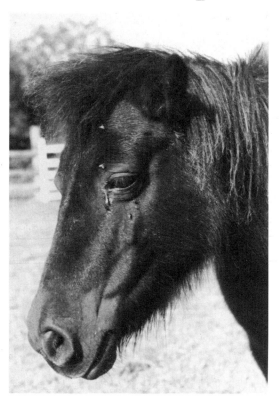

Flies cause immense irritation around the eyes as they are particularly attracted to the tears.

When using a fly fringe or nets in the field your horse will need to wear a headcollar. In the interests of safety it is best to use a 'Fieldsafe' headcollar, which is one that has soft rubber links; these allow the headcollar to break in the event of an emergency such as being caught on a fence or tree.

wounds are thoroughly cleaned and dry; bathe and dry them frequently for best effect. In addition, ensure that your horse's eyes, nose and dock are always kept clean and dry. Having accomplished this, you should set about making your horse a less desirable, place for flies to visit. You can regularly use an insecticidal or repellent product, and you may wish to couple this with the use of a fly fringe or net over the head to protect the eyes and ears.

Should your horse object to the application of a fly repellent spray, you should put it onto a sponge initially and then wipe it all over his body; but be careful of his eyes and nose.

Another fairly effective control measure is to use an insecticidal browband. This

from equine infectious anaemia, a disease which they can easily pass on.

Swift treatment with antiseptic or antibiotic creams is most effective for fly problems; however, it is far better to endeavour to control fly irritation in the first place.

Managing Fly Irritation

Fly bites can be tremendously annoying to horses during the summer months, causing painful bites which may result in swellings and intense skin irritation. To help prevent bites, make sure that any

The most effective way of controlling flies is to remove them from source: this means disturbing their breeding ground so that you can eradicate the majority of a whole new population. Many flies breed in and around a muck heap, so this is where you should start. If you keep a tidy, squared-off muck heap, this in itself will help to kill the flies, due to the heat that generates inside. You can also spray the heap daily with an insecticide to control those flies that settle on the top.

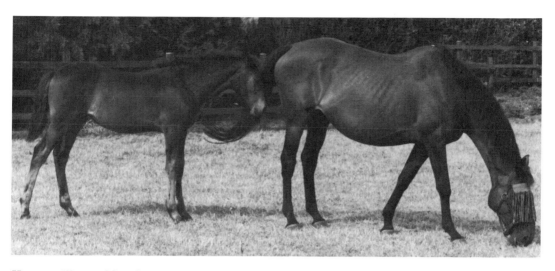

Horses will stand head to tail in order to swat flies from each other.

A fly fringe can be of immense benefit.

distributes insecticide over the horse's body and remains effective for up to about three weeks. Should your horse be particularly thin-skinned he may be troubled by flies more than most other horses, and in this instance he will benefit from the use of a summer sheet while turned out – but do remember to remove it should it rain.

Other Flies

Warbles

You will usually first notice signs of warbles in the saddle area, where the larvae can cause painful swellings. Once you notice anything untoward you must stop riding your horse as this will be extremely painful to him. You will then have to allow for a period where the larvae can migrate to the exterior, which can be encouraged by hot fomentation or applying poultices. It is important that you involve your vet as soon as possible; he may recommend surgical intervention to remove the warbles.

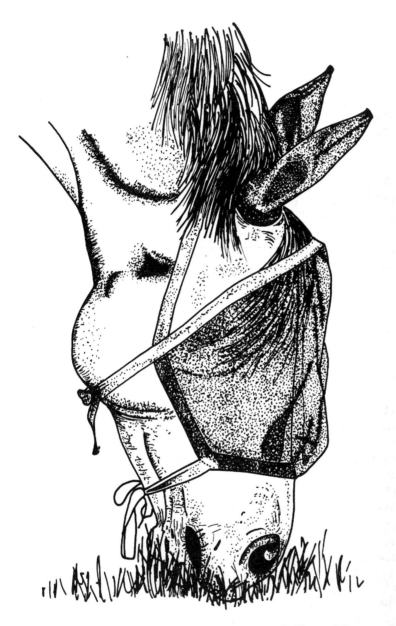

A fly net can protect a horse's eyes from fly irritation.

Other Parasites

Bots

These parasites are discussed fully in the section on Worms and their Life-Cycles.

Lice

Lice are small, dark-coloured parasites which can live on your horse all year

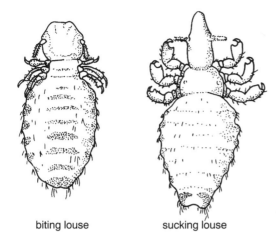

biting louse   sucking louse

Two types of lice commonly found on horses.

Sheep Ticks

Sheep ticks can be a real menace, although they are not that common. Once they find themselves on a horse they will bite into him and will not let go, even to the point where you can pull their bodies away from their jaws. Should you do this the horse is at risk from having an infected sore, which can take time to heal. They usually attach themselves to the horse's tummy and chest, although I have encountered them around the ears and face also. The only way to extract them 'whole' is to dope them so they will relax their jaws. To do this, soak a piece of cotton wool in methylated spirits and hold it over the whole tick for a minute or so; once intoxicated you can carefully lever it away from the horse's body.

Ringworm

Ringworm affects both stable- and grass-kept horses. It is not caused by a worm at all but by a fungus, and acquired its name because of the round bald patches which develop as a result of the condition – although in many cases, the bald patches are not even round.

Preventing ringworm is very difficult as it is highly contagious and has a long incubation period: your horse could have come into contact with a contagious horse three months earlier, and only just have developed the condition! Isolate him as soon as you realize he has ringworm. Treat the condition by using a topical antibiotic skin wash, usually applied three times at three-day intervals, and then again two weeks later if necessary. If the condition is established, treat with an antifungal antibiotic; certain of these you put in the feed for seven to ten days, although they must

round, and they love nothing better than to burrow into a long, muddy coat. They live and breed in natural debris such as skin grease, scurf and body fluids. Although they are visible to the naked eye, you may only realize that they are there when your horse starts to rub. Lice bite and suck the horse's blood which causes great irritation, and in some cases he will rub himself until bald patches occur. Lice are contagious so you should not allow your horse to come into contact with any others until you are certain you have eradicated them from his coat.

As soon as you notice lice, give your horse a thorough dusting with a good louse powder. This will need to be repeated at two-weekly intervals to kill off new parasites as they hatch out. Be especially vigilant in the cold months of the year as lice are then much more active than in hot weather. Although you cannot give your horse a thorough grooming if he is living out, you can check to make sure that nothing goes unnoticed.

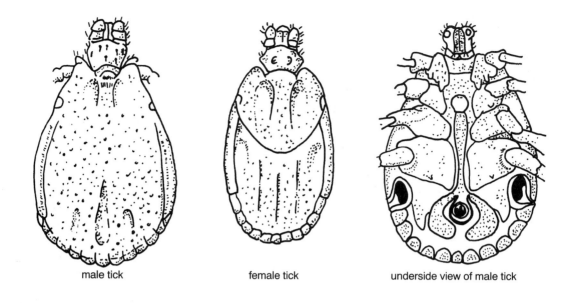

male tick   female tick   underside view of male tick

Identification of ticks.

not be used for broodmares. Ensure strict standards of hygiene by disinfecting all tack and shelters with a fungicidal solution, and do not touch other horses in the field without first disinfecting your own hands and clothes.

The first sign of ringworm may be no more than discreet little tufts of hair; however, these soon develop into raised patches that fall off easily and continue to do so until you see small hairless patches of crusty skin, which may or may not exude a small amount of serum. Ringworm commonly appears around the girth and saddle areas, but will often spread all over the body. Sometimes you will not observe any of the raised patches, but will just see the typical type of 'ring' appear and spread all over your horse's coat. Once these patches become dry and scaly, it will take about four weeks for the hair to regrow. You can encourage the hair to grow back strong and the right colour by rubbing in coconut oil.

CHAPTER 9

Health Care and Common Ailments

The grass-kept horse can be at risk to many different ailments. However, not many of them are serious and often a few basic precautions can prevent most of them from occurring in the first place.

Skin Ailments

Both winter and summer bring with them all sorts of potential problems for the horse, but whether they get out of hand can be due to either bad management or just plain bad luck. The trouble with many skin ailments is that they begin as harmless enough – a few scabs or a little patch of flaky skin are all that is to be seen – but if ignored at this stage, before you know it your horse is covered, which can mean weeks of treatment and huge vet bills. The message, then, is to be vigilant!

The horse's skin is his main defence against infection so it is very important that you keep it clean and healthy. If his skin becomes damaged there will be a weak point at which bacteria from the atmosphere can enter the body. The skin consists of many layers and although it is waterproof, it can be softened if it is continually damp, during a wet winter or spring for example. This can give rise to conditions such as mud fever and rainscald. Dry, hot weather can also bring its own problems, such as sweet-itch, and some skin conditions, such as ringworm, appear at any time of the year; so never let yourself become complacent.

Winter Skin Ailments

During the cold winter months mud fever, rain scald and cracked heels are all skin

All sorts of parasites love to bury themselves into a long-coated, ungroomed horse for the winter, and consequently they can cause a lot of damage underneath. So even if your horse has been turned away, still bring him in and give him a brush down with a dandy brush. This will ensure you detect any cuts or developing ailments and can take action immediately. During these regular grooming sessions always be on the look-out for any parasites or any patches of your horse's coat which look as though they have been rubbed.

Where a horse is known to be susceptible to mud fever, extreme vigilance is needed. Not only is mud fever very painful for the horse, it can also lead to more serious infections: for instance, if mud fever is left untreated, it can spread up the legs to the flexor tendons and cause serious lameness.

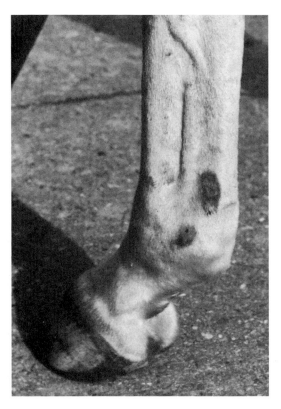

Do not be caught out: mud fever can flare up at any time, and horses in the middle of summer have been known to show mud fever symptoms.

complaints that can affect your horse. They are caused by a dermatitis bacterium (*Dermatophilus congolensis*) which thrives in damp, muddy conditions and produces scabby eczema-like symptoms which can be very painful for your horse. The condition is known as mud fever when the legs are affected, rain-scald when the back is affected and cracked heels when symptoms are shown in the hollows of the pasterns. Mud fever is recognized by scabby lesions which can become inflamed and very painful. If your horse has white legs he will be more prone

to it, and the pasterns are commonly affected. Cracked heels start as scurf and scabs in the hollow at the back of the pastern, which then develop into painful cracks. Rain-scald is recognized as raised tufts of hair with scurf surrounding them, over the back and rump.

Horses that are left standing for long periods in wet, muddy conditions are commonly affected, as extended soaking softens the skin and the abrasive action of mud then breaks it, enabling the bacterium to enter easily. The bacterium which causes mud fever forms spores that are capable of surviving on the horse's coat for many months, if not years. It can therefore flare up at any time and horses in the middle of summer have been known to show mud fever symptoms.

Prevention of Skin Ailments

Prevention of mud fever and its associated conditions is certainly better than cure. In winter it is a good idea to put shale down in front of gates and water troughs or wherever else horses gather, to prevent them from standing in vast areas of sloppy mud.

Keeping your horse dry and clean is of course desirable, but is really impossible to achieve with the horse living out. Applying a barrier cream such as zinc and castor oil or liquid paraffin to his heels and lower legs when he is dry, or before turning him out if he has been in for some reason, will help to protect susceptible areas. Try to encourage him to use his shelter as much as possible, by putting in plenty of hay and a deep, clean and dry bed.

Keep a close eye on your horse, checking him every day when you bring him in for grooming. It is a good idea to clean the mud off his legs each time, preferably by allowing it to dry and then brushing it off. Do this gently, because vigorous brushing with coarse bristles can cause more of the abrasions which allow the mud fever bacteria to enter. However, few of us have time to wait for mud to dry, so hosing is usually the only course of action. If you need to hose mud off his legs, be sure you dry them gently but thoroughly afterwards.

Treatment

At the very first sign of infection you must begin treatment. The first thing to do if your horse shows signs of mud fever or cracked heels is to eliminate the cause, so he should be taken off the paddock. If there are only one or two horses in the field, you can make good use of the field shelter by putting slip rails across the front. This allows the horse to enjoy the view and still walk around to some extent, where the alternative would be either to shut him in a stable or to yard him.

To treat mud fever once it has become established, first clip away any long hair from around the affected area and gently remove the scabs to expose the condition to the air. These scabs will be hard and crusty, and removal of them may be extremely painful for your horse. To minimize the pain, first moisten the scabs by washing with an antibacterial soap and warm water.

If mud fever has been left unmanaged, a horse's legs may be covered with scabs. You may need to soak each affected leg either by simply hosing it, by using a hose boot, or by tubbing with warm water for at least half an hour before trying to remove them. Dry thoroughly by gently patting with clean gamgee. More severe cases may need warm poulticing before you attempt to remove the scabs, as secondary bacterial infection often

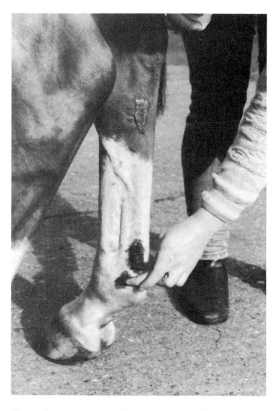

Once the scabs have been removed, the area will be very sore, so apply a soothing antibiotic ointment, twice daily.

develops. Squeeze the poultice as much as possible in order to draw out the infection and any remaining dirt; the warmth will also help to increase blood supply to the damaged area which will promote healing and reduce inflammation. Once the poultice is removed, the condition can be treated as before. Where a secondary bacterial infection has developed a course of antibiotics may be needed.

Once the scabs have been removed the area will be very sore, so apply a soothing antibiotic ointment twice daily; certain of these ointments contain corticosteroid, and they help in reducing any inflammation which may be a factor in more severe cases of the condition. Within a few days the condition will start to dry up and new hair will already be starting to grow.

Rain-Scald

When the horse is left unrugged and without shelter from the rain he is quite likely to develop rain-scald. Long periods of driving rain allow the dermatophilus bacteria to penetrate the softened skin. At first you will notice that the coat is beginning to look 'stary' and clumps of hair will be starting to rise away from the skin; this is more obvious over the back, loins, shoulder and quarters. 'Paintbrush' lesions then occur, large tufts of hair which become matted together. Once these have developed they can be picked off, the lesions washed with an antibacterial soap and left to dry, as with mud fever. Your horse will need to be shut into his shelter or stable until the condition has healed, and in the future you will always have to put a waterproof rug on him during the winter, as once a horse has suffered from the condition he will be more susceptible.

Chapped Face

Where a horse is out during windy weather he may develop runny eyes. This may not be too much of a problem in itself, as it will usually stop once the wind drops. However, the horse can easily get a chapped face if left to fend for himself in prolonged windy conditions. First of all you need to sponge the face daily with a warm, damp sponge to remove any discharge. Then you should dry the area thoroughly and apply a protective layer of petroleum jelly, or an antiseptic cream if an infection has set in. Make sure that your horse has adequate shelter so that he can get out of the wind if he wants to.

Summer Skin Ailments

Sweet-Itch

Just as the threat from mud fever starts to abate, you begin to worry about summer ailments! Sweet-itch is a condition caused by a reaction to the saliva of biting midges which are prevalent from spring until autumn, and which cause horses to rub their manes and tails. The severity of the condition varies from horse to horse; some will only rub occasionally, while others will rub themselves bald, causing open sores.

Rather than waiting to treat it once it has occurred, this is certainly a condition which should be prevented at all costs. If possible make sure your horse is shut into his shelter around dusk and dawn as the midges that cause the trouble are more active around these times. If you cannot do this there are other measures that you can take in order to protect your horse:

1. Use a summer sheet on your horse during dry, hot weather but make sure it is secure.
2. Use a linen hood, which covers half the head and the mane, and a linen tail guard or a 'tail-tidy' from 3.30 pm to 8.30 am.
3. Prevent your horse from grazing areas that have ponds nearby, as these naturally attract the troublesome midges.
4. Feed garlic as this helps to keep the midges off.
5. Use a long-acting fly repellent, all over the body.

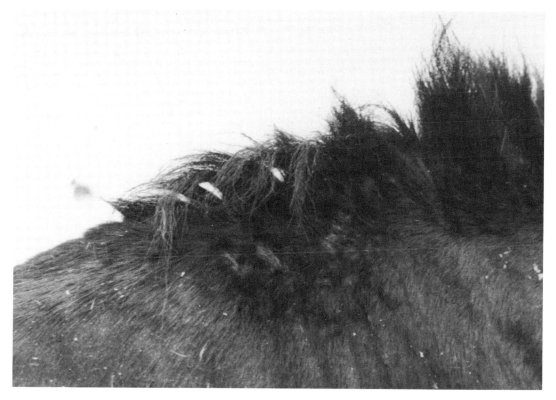

Sweet-itch is a condition caused by a reaction to the saliva of biting midges, which are prevalent from spring to autumn, and which causes horses to rub their manes.

Begin to treat sweet-itch immediately you see any sign of it. Obtain a good spray-on shampoo from your vet, and when washing the mane and tail rub it well in to help remove any scurf and scabs. Rinse it out thoroughly, or your horse might then start rubbing as a result of shampoo irritation. Wash your horse with this shampoo every week while he is suffering, and apply a soothing lotion afterwards; as well as offering relief, such a lotion will also help to discourage the midges from biting. Rub it well in to all areas twice daily, including the underside of the mane and tail.

Sunburn and Photosensitization

Sunburn occurs after the commencement of a period of hot, sunny weather; it particularly affects ponies with white markings, and especially their muzzle. Photosensitization also occurs during the summer months, mostly affecting horses with unpigmented skin which also have white areas on the legs and face; typically chestnuts with white hair on their legs or face overlying pink skin, greys and skewbald and piebald horses are susceptible. The likely cause is that

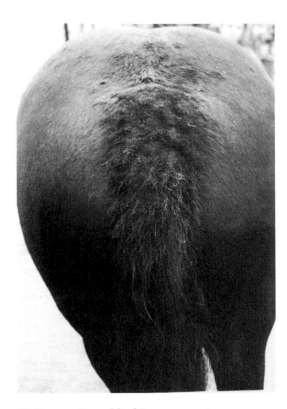

Tails are also rubbed in response to midges.

and apply barrier creams, but in all cases it is sensible to have a correct veterinary diagnosis in the first place. Similarly, for sunburn it is best to stable your horse during the day and only turn him out at night, or in cloudy, dull weather.

Urticaria

Urticaria has various causes and is commonly known as nettle rash, or hives. The most common causes are thought to be a reaction:

- to biting flies;
- to something in the horse's diet, perhaps barley;
- to nettles or irritating undergrowth;
- to various drugs.

At first you will see raised patches of fluid under the skin varying in size and number. The condition is a little puzzling, in that these patches may develop and disappear within hours, or they may be more persistent. The only sensible course of action is to pinpoint the cause and avoid contact with it in the future. If the conditions seems to be troubling your horse, or the patches are severe, call your vet who will be able to prescribe the appropriate drugs for a speedier recovery.

First Aid Treatment

the horse has eaten phototoxic plants (such as St John's Wort), or – although these causes are less usual – that he has some form of liver disease, or has reacted to a thiabendazole wormer or trifoliates in hay or pasture. It would appear that although the two constant factors of pink, unpigmented skin and exposure to sunlight are necessary, there needs to be a third 'trigger' factor as a causative agent in order for an initial attack to occur. However, once the horse has succumbed once it seems that any one of the three factors can trigger off an attack.

You will first notice the skin becoming crusty, with layers peeling off. You should stable your horse during sunny weather

By far the most common injuries that you will have to deal with in the horse at grass are wounds, cuts and minor grazes: this alone is a good reason for your horse having regular tetanus boosters. To prevent further complications you must deal with any cut quickly and efficiently. The first sign of trouble that you may notice is blood trickling down from the injured site, so you should

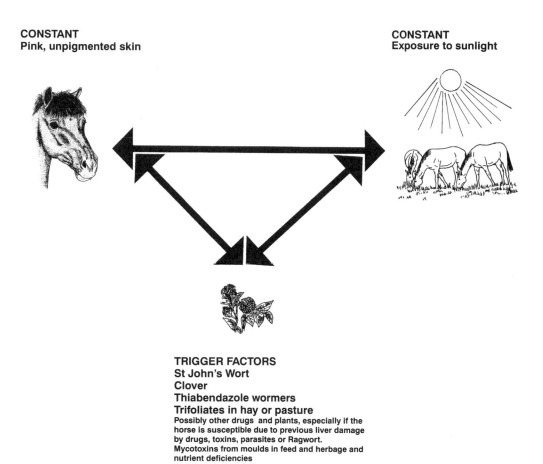

CONSTANT
Pink, unpigmented skin

CONSTANT
Exposure to sunlight

TRIGGER FACTORS
St John's Wort
Clover
Thiabendazole wormers
Trifoliates in hay or pasture
Possibly other drugs and plants, especially if the horse is susceptible due to previous liver damage by drugs, toxins, parasites or Ragwort. Mycotoxins from moulds in feed and herbage and nutrient deficiencies

The causative agents of photosensitization.

catch your horse and assess the damage immediately. As a rule a minor wound will stop bleeding by itself within a few minutes so there is no need to panic, but immediate action is required for anything more serious.

Your first priority is to stop the flow of blood, especially if the horse appears to have severed an artery; you can assume this is the case if you can see bright red blood spurting from the injury. If it is clear that the blood is coming from a single artery, apply pressure using your thumb,

You should always call the vet in the following circumstances: if the wound is spurting blood; if it needs stitching: if it is deep and/or more than one inch (2.5cm) long, for example; if the affected area swells up more than a little; if your horse has not been vaccinated against tetanus; if the wound is leaking joint oil; if for any other reason you are at all worried about the injury.

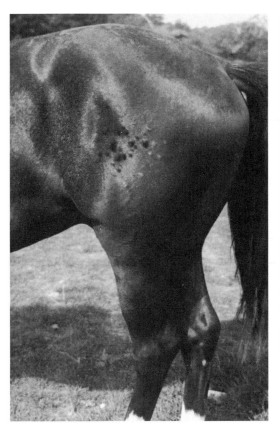

Urticaria has various causes and is commonly known as nettle rash, or hives.

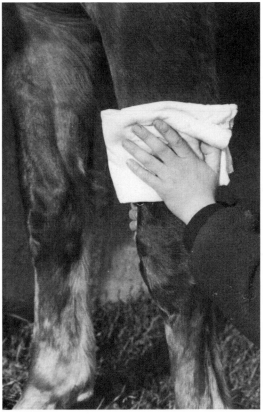

In order to stop the blood from any injury, hold a pad of clean material firmly over the wound and apply pressure.

about an inch (2.5cm) along the artery above the wound, to arrest the flow. In order to stop the blood from other injuries, hold a pad of clean material (gamgee is fine if it is ready to hand; if not you can improvise by using a clean handkerchief) firmly over the wound and again apply pressure. If you feel your horse needs a vet call him and tell him what is happening.

Keep applying pressure to the pad, and if blood soaks through simply apply another gamgee pad over the top. Once the bleeding lessens, the pad/s can be bandaged firmly and evenly over the area until the vet arrives. If you can bring your horse into a stable without starting the bleeding again do so, otherwise try to keep him still where he is.

Less serious wounds still need attention, but may be attended to by yourself if you are experienced enough.

Cleansing Wounds

To have the best chance of a good recovery every wound needs to be well cleaned, however minor it may appear. Often the flow of blood itself is enough to clean it, but in minor wounds, any visible dirt can be carefully removed and the wound further cleaned with a swab soaked in warm salty water (about one teaspoon of salt to one pint of water). Using a clean swab each time, always work from the middle outwards. Run a hosepipe above the area if dirt is still present, so that a gentle trickle of water removes it and any congealed blood. Do not apply water pressure to the wound as this will drive any foreign bodies further into the broken flesh.

After cleaning, minor cuts should be left to dry and then treated sparingly with an antiseptic powder or spray. You can turn your horse back out, as long as you bring him back in to repeat the process three times daily until the wound has dried up.

If, having brought your horse in from the field and after cleaning the wound it becomes obvious that it needs stitching, cover it with a clean piece of gamgee, bandage this in place and call your vet. Do not put on any healing creams, powders, sprays or gels as this will only hinder the vet.

More serious wounds will need dressing, and a badly infected wound may need poulticing to draw out dirt and infection. If it is not infected, apply a lint wound dressing directly onto the wound, cover with a piece of gamgee, and if possible bandage into place over another layer of gamgee; if the damage is on a leg, this should extend all the way down the leg. Obviously a horse with such a wound cannot be turned out, although there is nothing to stop you employing a yarding procedure if you have the necessary facilities. To prevent other areas from becoming infected, you can use large sticky plasters, although these will need to be replaced regularly.

Hoof and Foot Conditions

Hoof Cracks

Cracks in the hoof wall can be common in horses kept at grass, especially if the feet have been at all neglected. Such cracks do not require emergency treatment but they do need prompt attention by your farrier if they are not to get worse and cause lameness. There are two main types of cracks: those which start at the ground and work upwards, known as grass cracks; and those which start at the coronary band and work downwards, known as sandcracks.

In the majority of cases these cracks only involve the outer horn, so as long as they are dealt with promptly and correctly your horse should remain sound. However, if the crack goes deeper, into the sensitive laminae, or if these tissues have become infected, your horse is likely to go lame. In some cases you may see pus draining out of the hoof, which will then require poulticing before any corrective action can be taken by your vet or farrier.

Punctured Soles

Punctured soles are very common in the grass-kept horse, often caused by the horse standing on a sharp object such as a nail or flint. All puncture wounds should be taken seriously, as the wound can heal over on the surface and/or become infected underneath, creating pus that forms a painful abscess; so during your daily observations always be sure to pick up the feet for a closer examination. Tetanus as a consequence of this sort of injury is also a risk, so call your vet for all but the most superficial of such wounds.

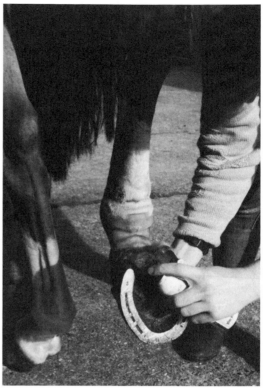

To prevent infection, a punctured sole needs to be treated by washing off any dirt and mud and then dipping the foot into a solution of salt water or mild antiseptic.

In a case of thrush, clean and scrub the foot out daily, and once dry, apply an antiseptic spray.

You may suspect a punctured sole for two reasons:

1. Your horse may come hobbling across the field towards you with an offending item still in his hoof.

2. Your horse will suddenly go very lame. Obviously you will need to remove any evident item straightaway but be careful to prevent further damage. Once it is removed, a hole is usually clearly visible. To prevent infection this needs to be treated by washing off any dirt and mud and then dipping the foot into a solution of salt water or mild antiseptic to help kill any infection. To keep the area clean, cover it for a few days. If you use a well fitting 'easy-boot' you will still be able to turn your horse out, but keep a regular check on him and make sure that no infection is present before turning him out again without it.

If your horse is very lame, then his foot is more than likely infected and your vet should be called as he may need to cut a hole in the sole to allow the pus to drain out. If you poultice the foot before your vet arrives this will help to soften the sole and draw the pus down so it will run out freely when the outer horn is cut away.

Thrush

Thrush is a condition where the frog appears spongy and wet, and there is a foul-smelling black discharge. It usually occurs in the stabled horse as a result of him being obliged to stand on dirty, wet bedding for long periods of time, especially where the feet are not picked out regularly. However, it can equally affect a horse that stands in similar conditions in the field shelter. First, clear out the old bedding and keep the shelter dry and clean in the future. Clean and scrub out the foot daily, and once it is dry, spray on an antiseptic spray. To protect the foot from wet bedding apply a barrier cream or preparation, such as Stockholm tar. Thrush will usually clear up rapidly once treated and the cause removed. However, if the condition has been neglected to such an extent that the sensitive laminae have been affected, then the foot will need to be poulticed and treated by your vet.

Bruised Soles

Bruised sole is a common cause of lameness in grass-kept horses, and usually results from the horse standing on a sharp object such as a flint. In a severe case an abscess may result which will need poulticing, and then paring by your vet. On removal of the shoe, examination may reveal a corn (a bruise in the heel region). If this is the case, it will need to be cut out. A special surgical shoe may be fitted to relieve the pressure of corns. If your horse is particularly thin-soled, it would be sensible to ask your farrier about fitting a leather pad under the shoe for future protection.

Laminitis

Laminitis is notoriously suffered by ponies grazing lush spring grass; however there can be a variety of other causes, such as over-feeding or changes in diet. It is a very painful condition that usually affects only the front feet, although only one or all of the feet can be affected. Although ponies suffer more frequently, it can affect horses of all ages and sizes.

Symptoms which might lead you to believe your horse has laminitis include:
- the 'laminitic stance', where the horse stands with the forelegs stretched forwards;
- he refuses to move;
- he objects to having the sole tested with pinchers;

In order to prevent laminitis in a susceptible horse always try to eliminate possible causes: keep him off grass, or reduce his feed, for example. This does not necessarily mean you need to bring your horse in from the paddock; you can put him out onto a bare piece of land, in which case he will need the addition of hay to ensure his digestive system still functions properly, or you can put on a muzzle, removing it for short periods to allow him to graze. Alternatively you can cut small holes into the bottom of a leather muzzle (probably the best idea as the horse can drink and the holes provide good ventilation). Also they will allow just a few blades of grass to poke through at a time, but in so organizing things you are mimicking the horse's natural way of life, as he will be having to work far harder for less food.

Typical laminitis stance.

- there is heat in the affected feet;
- there are rings on the feet which indicate that the horse has suffered in the past;
- he may have a raised temperature, pulse and respiration rate due to the pain.

Laminitis should always be treated as an emergency. Early treatment very often leads to a more successful outcome, so the vet should be called without delay. If the onset is sudden, you can hose the feet with cold water while waiting for the vet as this will offer your horse some relief from the pain. However, do not give painkilling drugs, as these will mask the severity of the condition.

As a long-term measure, corrective trimming will often be necessary, so your farrier should become involved. In addition, ask your vet about future exercise and feeding and follow his recommendations closely. Once suffered, laminitis is likely to recur so you need to make a commitment to your horse's future management.

To prevent recurrence by only allowing limited grazing at times of plenty is usually the most effective method. However, you should not 'starve' your horse as this will cause its own problems. Instead offer a low nutritional alternative, such as average meadow hay.

To control laminitis you can put your horse out onto a bare piece of land.

Other Illnesses

Grass Sickness

Grass sickness is a fatal condition, but fortunately it is rare. It is a very traumatic disease of the nervous system, which affects the horse's alimentary canal.

There is no cure, and the only way to proceed after diagnosis is to have your horse quickly put down to prevent further suffering. Symptoms include: depression, rapid pulse, rapid weight loss, inability to swallow food or water, dehydration, food regurgitated and running from both nostrils, lack of gut sounds and severe colic.

Poisoning

Horses are very good at selecting an appropriate diet for themselves as long as one is on offer. Thankfully they are able to distinguish between beneficial and harmful plants so poisoning is rare. However, if there is little else for the horse to eat, he may be forced to consume what he knows is bad for him, resulting in poisoning. The main causes of poisoning are that your horse has:

• eaten a poisonous plant (see Chapter 5);
• been fed contaminated food;
• licked something poisonous, perhaps a newly treated gate or fence;

Laminitis can also be controlled by muzzling, cutting small holes into the bottom of the leather muzzle to allow just a few blades of grass to poke through at a time.

- accidentally been given an overdose of drugs;
- been 'nobbled' – deliberately poisoned;
- or that he is one of the unlikely horses that react badly to bee, wasp or hornet stings.

Although horses have a very delicate sense of smell and taste and most will spit out something which does not taste right, it is obviously best to ensure that there is nothing poisonous in the horse's field, hay, feed or stable.

In mild cases a poisoned horse may show signs very similar to those of colic (see next section); in serious cases he can die within minutes of having eaten something highly poisonous, although this is rare. If you suspect poisoning, call your vet immediately.

Colic

Colic is a term used to describe abdominal pain which comes from the digestive system, or, in the case of renal colic, from the kidneys. It can vary from a mild case to an extremely painful and distressing one. Should you discover your horse acting oddly in the field, a prime suspect for the cause is colic. Horses suffer from colic more than any other animal, and it can be caused by various anomalies when the horse is kept at grass:

1. Worm infestation: this may be because the horse's worming programme has been neglected, or he has been give an inappropriate type of wormer for the time of year.
2. Irregular feeding: where a horse is fed concentrates in the field you should keep to a routine in the same way as you would with the stabled horse.
3. Drinking large quantities of cold water while the horse is still hot: this can happen if immediately you return from a tiring ride you turn your horse straight out into the field, before allowing him to cool down.
4. Sudden changes of diet: where a horse is suddenly put onto lush grass, or taken off grass and put onto concentrates.
5. Poor quality food: food that is mouldy or dusty can cause colic.

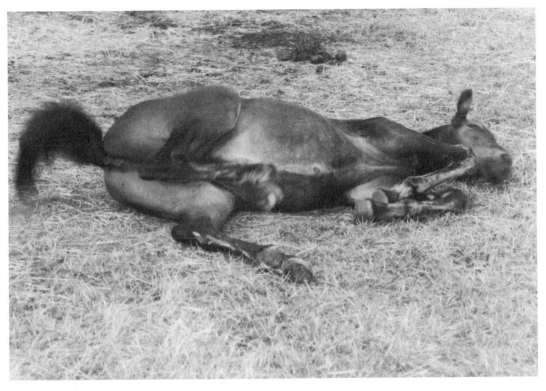

Should you discover your horse acting oddly in the field, a prime suspect for the cause is colic.

6. Incomplete mastication of food due to poor teeth: this is especially pertinent for older and younger horses, although not limited to them.

7. Anxiety or stress: this can happen if field companions are removed, thus leaving the horse alone.

Signs of Colic

Your horse will be generally uneasy, possibly sweating, and will often look towards his stomach and perhaps try to kick at it with his hind legs. He may be standing, or lying down or rolling violently, or repeatedly getting up and down. He may paw the ground or try to rub his tail on fences in an attempt to relieve the discomfort. He may find urinating difficult, passing only small amounts or none at all, and similarly with droppings.

If you suspect colic, do not give your horse anything to eat, or a colic drench. First take his temperature: with colic it does not usually rise above normal. Next check his pulse, which may rise in relation to the amount of pain he is experiencing. Horses usually find their own way of dealing with the pain from colic: they may simply find a comfortable position when lying down, they may roll or pace about. If your horse is lying down but not rolling, do not get him up, as this is his way of dealing with the pain. If he seems to be in only mild pain and is finding relief

In a case of colic always call your vet as an emergency measure if:
- the pulse exceeds 45–50;
- the eye membranes are deeper than a salmon pink or the colour that is normal for your horse;
- your horse does not find any relief from what appears to be a mild attack, within half-an-hour to an hour;
- he is obviously distressed or violent;
- he is rolling violently;
- he is attempting to pass urine or droppings, but cannot.

quickly, then do not panic, but keep a close eye on him until he starts to urinate or pass droppings freely, or stops showing signs of pain. However, if he does not start to improve quickly then it is better to call the vet sooner rather than later.

Having examined your horse, the vet may simply give him a pain-killer until the whole episode passes. And if more serious treatment is required he will be the best person to advise you.

Chronic Obstructive Pulmonary Disease (COPD)

COPD, often known as broken wind, is probably the most common cause of chronic coughing in horses. However, as it is caused by an allergy to stable dust and/or fungal spores in hay and straw it is rarely suffered by horses at grass. Indeed, turning the horse out is one of the solutions as it provides the ultimate 'clean air regime'. Once your horse is diagnosed as having COPD he should be turned out as much as possible; in fact all the time is the ideal. In winter, your horse will obviously need rugging and access to a shelter to protect him from adverse weather conditions, especially if he has usually lived in.

Pasture-Associated Pulmonary Disease (PAPD)

Some horses show signs of COPD while out at grass. This is thought to be caused by an allergic reaction to certain pollens and is known as PAPD. Oilseed rape has been suspected as a possible cause of this condition, although there is no scientific proof to substantiate this. If your horse shows sign of PAPD while out at grass then you should try to prevent further sensitization to pollens by keeping him away from them as much as possible.

Glandular Swellings

These are mump-like swellings of the parotid salivary glands, situated behind the jaw, just below each ear. They always occur in horses at grass and seem to be restricted to the grazing of certain pastures. I personally had no knowledge of this condition until I bought a new horse a few years ago; having turned her out for a day, she came in looking as though she had done ten rounds with a heavyweight boxer! I was quite alarmed so telephoned my vet immediately, who also had no knowledge of the condition! Fortunately, although it looks dramatic it causes few problems other than facial swelling due to the enlarged glands obstructing drainage from the head. The precise cause is unknown, but it is assumed to be caused by an allergic reaction to some factor in certain types of grass or other plants. Only certain horses are affected, and in my case it was only this one mare on a paddock which dozens of other horses had grazed without problem.

There is no recommended treatment, although the swellings do reduce when the horse is brought indoors. Should this not be the case you should contact your veterinary surgeon immediately to obtain a correct diagnosis. My mare's condition resolved itself over a period of three months, so I can only assume that she got used to whatever caused it in the first place. To the untrained eye glandular swellings can appear indistinguishable to other conditions that necessitate urgent treatment, so it is sensible to contact your veterinary surgeon in the first instance.

Equine Influenza

If you suspect your horse is suffering from 'flu you should isolate him from the rest of the field immediately. Signs to look for are:
- a raised temperature, which may be anything between 101.5–106°F.
- a loss of appetite;
- a dry, rasping cough;
- a watery discharge, or a thicker more discoloured one if your horse has been suffering for some days;
- enlarged glands;
- watery or weeping eyes;
- shivering.

The first thing to do is to bring your horse in, as he needs to be kept warm. Put him in a stable with a good deep bed, rug

It is very important that all horses living together in a field are vaccinated regularly. If all owners act responsibly and have all their horses vaccinated, then far fewer horses will ever suffer from this infectious disease. To begin with your horse will need to have an initial course followed by yearly boosters.

him up and put on stable bandages. Try to prevent any draughts, but ensure that there is still plenty of ventilation. You should call your vet, so that he can examine your horse and give an accurate diagnosis. Once your horse's temperature has gone down he will benefit from being turned back out, although he still needs to be kept warm.

Pneumonia

Pneumonia is uncommon in adult horses, but it is a mistake to think that it only happens as a development of 'flu. Pneumonia can develop as a result of colic drenches being inhaled, which is why vets no longer recommend their use. The signs of pneumonia are similar to those of flu, but additionally your horse may be breathing faster and his condition may drop rapidly. Always call the vet if you suspect pneumonia, and while waiting, keep your horse warm and stay with him for company.

Hypothermia

Hypothermia is caused when the horse's body temperature drops well below normal and is not able to recover. If a horse is not treated efficiently he will not survive, so immediate action must be taken. Don't be fooled into thinking it is only old or finely-bred horses that can succumb: *all* horses are potential sufferers, even those of the most hardy breeds if they are exposed to the causes. These are insufficient food, combined with freezing winds and icy rain, and no shelter.

You should suspect hypothermia if your horse is lethargic, and showing no interest in his surroundings; is looking completely miserable; appears tucked up; if his coat is standing on end and he is shivering, or feels cold under the dock, behind the elbow or at the base of the ears. Horses with hypothermia will lose weight rapidly.

You must warm the horse up as soon as possible: bring him in, rug him up, put on stable bandages and provide a nice thick bed. Walking around in an indoor school will help to promote circulation, or you could employ the use of infra-red lamps. Call the vet to see what he can do.

In future you must prevent your horse from ever suffering again by ensuring he has all the feed he needs, suitable shelter and warmth.

Sinus Infections

On either side of his head the horse has large frontal sinuses, which drain straight into his nasal cavity. If these sinuses become infected, your horse might seem a

---

Administering Drugs to the Horse in a Field

When administering drugs to a field-kept horse it is best to use either oral pastes or injections. Putting powders in the food is not always that effective, as you can never be sure that the horse had received the full amount. He may kick his feed bowl over, or worse, another horse may eat the feed. With pastes and injections you can be safe in the knowledge that the horse has received all you intended to give.

---

little head-shy and you will see a thick discharge coming down one or other of his nostrils. Usually a course of antibiotics from your vet will clear up the problem; also feeding your horse from the floor will help the sinuses to drain and thus prevent them from becoming blocked again.

CHAPTER 10

Safety and Insurance

Safeguarding your Horse and Equipment

Horse theft is unfortunately a thriving and lucrative industry, with no emotional feelings on the thief's part. No matter how loved or cherished an animal, or how much it is worth, a thief will steal it if it is physically possible. Sadly these days it is quite easy, especially when many people are of the opinion it won't happen to them. It does not matter to horse thieves whether your horse is a top show jumper or a brood mare. It is still a horse and to thieves that means money. Horse stealing is no longer an opportunist industry, it is a highly organized world, in which unscrupulous people will do anything to get their hands on

horses which they know will earn them a nice amount of money. Today your horse could be quietly munching in his field and tomorrow he could be on the other side of the country, or even abroad.

Stealing horses is big business and it is not only a male occupation. In fact, a horse thief is just as likely to be a woman. Thieves no longer come upon a horse by chance and decide to take him. The whole thing is planned in advance. They often steal to order, scouring the countryside for the horse they know will have a buyer. Having found a good candidate they will observe how he is kept, when his owner visits him and how good he is to handle all without you being aware of their presence. Therefore, you have to make it as

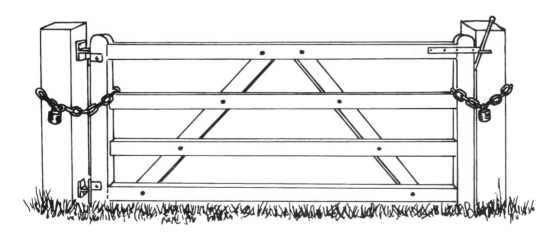

Lock both ends of the gate.

difficult as possible for the thieves to steal your horse. In reality, every horse is a potential target so action must be taken now, before you walk to the paddock and get that sinking feeling in your stomach as you realize you horse is missing. Is your horse being targeted right now? Are you aware? What should you do?

Field Security

It is very much down to you to provide maximum security for your horse. All horses turned out into fields need protection, especially if they live out all the time. Thieves will have observed that they live out and will wait until the time is right to pounce.

Sometimes a deterrent is all that is needed. First, the field gate should be padlocked at both ends; there is little use just padlocking one end, as the gate can then be quietly and simply lifted off its hinges at the other. Heavy-duty chains will certainly make a thief think twice before attempting to cut the metal, so use these where possible.

Electric fencing may provide a deterrent to opportunist thieves.

There are alarms available on the market that are triggered by the action of the gate opening – though you or someone else must be within earshot, and preferably sight, of the field. It is inadvisable to keep your horse in an isolated field away from your home; these remotely placed horses are easy prey for the discerning thief. Also be aware that horses are not only taken at night time, so the alarm and locks should always be on whenever horses are in the field.

Electric fencing may provide a deterrent to opportunist thieves, if they unexpectedly get a shock. However, it is not a fail-safe system as professional thieves will come prepared with rubber gloves and wire cutters. If the gate leads out onto a road, try to re-site it if possible where it is in view of some houses or the yard.

It is a good idea to visit your horse as early in the morning and as late at night as possible. Try to ensure there is no set routine or pattern, so anyone 'casing' the area for a suitable horse can see you arriving at different times. Keep a look out for any dubious looking people, especially if they stop outside your field on more than one occasion. Any suspicious behaviour should be reported to the police, along with relevant descriptions and number plates. A crime prevention officer, who can be contacted through the local police station, will be pleased to offer advice on securing your premises and on local crime prevention schemes (see pages 155–156).

Security lighting will deter thieves or may well cause them to fail in their attempts to steal your horse.

Security Lighting

Security lighting will also deter thieves or may well cause them to fail in their attempts to steal your horse. A passive infra-red detector will be invisible to the thief until he walks through the detector beam, when the flood lights will be turned on. These are much safer and better for your horse, than leaving floodlights on all night staring out into the field.

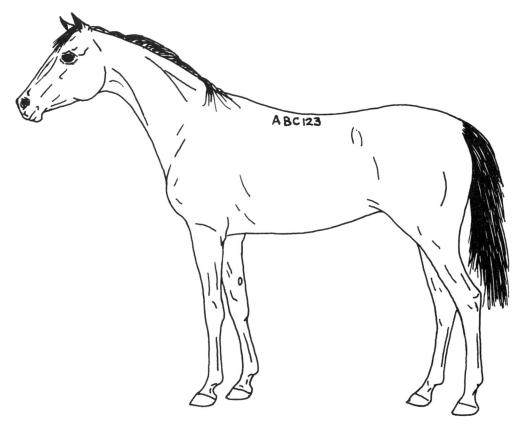

Methods of identification: freeze-marking.

Deterrents

Freeze-Marking

The best known deterrent is freeze-marking, where a permanent mark is applied to the horse's skin with a chilled branding iron. Contrary to popular belief, it will not hurt your horse, and should not affect your chances in the show ring. The mark is applied to a clipped area of your horse's back on the saddle patch, and the pigment cells in the hair are destroyed, growing back white within a few weeks. Grey or light-coloured horses are marked in the same way, but the mark stays bald. For this reason, the area on grey horses may need regular clipping so the freeze-mark is apparent. If your horse gets sold on, he will be easier to trace if freeze-marked. Many insurance companies offer premium reductions if this has been done, as the chances of tracing a stolen horse without a freeze-mark are slim.

Rather than having a random number used on their horse some owners prefer to have their own identifying mark, such as their initials. If you would prefer this you should check that the company will allow

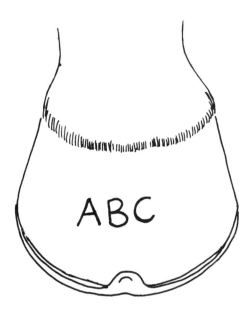 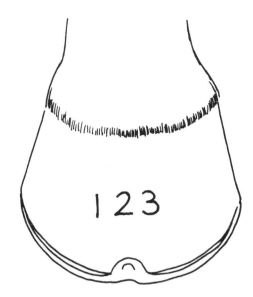

Methods of identification: hoof branding.

it and that the mark you want has not been allocated before.

Remember to keep the hair over the freeze-mark clipped off during the winter, or else it may be barely legible. Another good tip is to paint the freeze mark over the top of your rug. This leaves a thief in no doubt about what is underneath and may deter him from taking your horse. Of course, it is also a good way of identifying your rugs if stolen – or 'borrowed' – by other owners in a livery yard.

Other Deterrents

Other deterrents include *hoof branding*, a painless technique where the farrier burns an identification code, often your postcode, into your horse's hooves. You will need to have this form of identifica-tion redone at least twice a year, as the brand will grow out with the hoof.

Identichipping is another means of identifying a horse. A small microchip is injected under the horse's skin, carrying an identification code. When scanned, the code is traced, via a scanner network. Though not visible to a thief, this form of identification is very useful. The network of scanners spreads across major sale rings, and slaughter houses where the meat is sold for human consumption. Horsewatch co-ordinators and crime prevention officers are also aware of this method of identifying stolen horses and scanners are supplied on free loan to other establishments and personnel who require them for possible identification of lost or stolen horses. Notices are put on the field gates and fences to alert people that the horses have been protected in

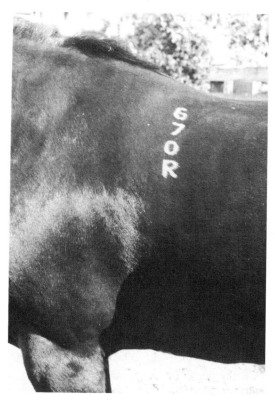

The best known deterrent to horse theft is freeze-marking.

Should your horse be stolen, the police will be able to identify it more easily if you have a description chart showing your horse's distinguishing marks and features. These should include facial markings, socks and stockings, whorls, scars, and marks on the hooves. A set of clear colour photographs showing these markings from both sides and front and rear will help the police identification process immensely, especially if taken in winter and summer, as the difference in coat and colour can vary through the seasons. A policeman may not be able to tell what a white blaze on a horse's face should look like, but a photograph will leave no doubt, enabling him to quickly match up marks exactly. Also remember to include the hooves, as white or dark hooves will help to identify your horse, if nothing else can.

this way, and there are also small tags for the headcollar.

Making a Horse Identity Certificate

You should ensure that everything you own relating to your horse is identifiable as your own property. This should include your horse box or trailer as well as your horse and his and your own equipment. In the event that stolen goods are recovered you will be reunited with your possessions far more quickly if you can prove ownership.

Trailers

If at all possible your trailer or horsebox should be kept out of sight, or in a locked building. This is rarely practical, though, and most trailers are kept in a field near the horse. You must make every effort to secure them in other ways – a wheel clamp or a steering wheel lock are very good security methods, as is security marking. Check with your insurance company whether or not your trailer is covered if kept outside, as there may be a loophole whereby only trailers in locked buildings are covered. There may even be a stipulation on what type of lock you use, as some padlocks are not considered secure enough.

Tack

Tack can be marked with your postcode, by means of metal identity punches; it can also be identichipped. Again, take

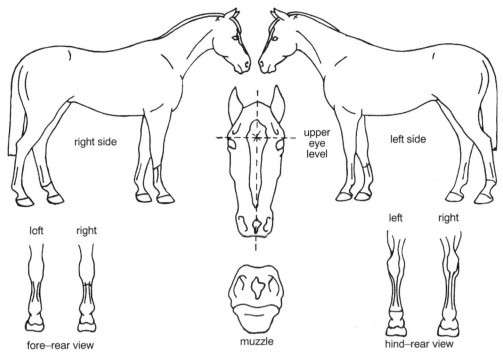

right side

upper
eye
level

left side

loft   right

left   right

fore—rear view

muzzle

hind—rear view

Make a diagram of your horse's markings.

photographs so that there can be no confusion over identity.

Enlisting Help

To help in the fight against equestrian crime, enlist the help of friends and neighbours. Let them know if you are going away, and ask them to keep a look out. If your horse's field is not adjacent to a yard, you would be better off moving him to a livery yard while you are away, to be on the safe side. Likewise, if the yard/field owners where your horse is kept will not be available for a while, make even more regular checks on him, or arrange for someone to stay at the yard and house-sit. This is a recognized service, and equestrian minded people often look after properties and animals while the owners are away.

In many countries there are now specialist equestrian crime units. As thieves often have a wide network, these crime units can liaise with other police forces to help track horses from one county, or possibly even from one country, to another.

Taking Action

What to do if your Horse / Tack is Stolen

Speed is absolutely vital if you are to have the greatest chance of recovery. Always telephone the police and make local enquiries to see if anyone saw or heard anything suspicious. If your horse is freeze-marked let the company know so it can alert auctioneers and ports. You could also try:

• Ask the police to arrange for sales in other areas to be checked.
• Check auctions being held the next day or in that week, as thieves often steal a horse they have had their eye on the night before, having already booked it into a sale.
• Telephone slaughter houses and give them a description of your horse.
• Keep on checking sales, if possible up and down the country. The British Horse Society or relevant governing body for your country will supply you with a list of sales and auctions if you send them a large stamped addressed envelope.
• Ask trade magazines and papers if they will publish news of the theft.
• Inform radio stations and ask them to broadcast the message, giving a description of your horse.
• Put up posters and details in riding schools and livery yards and in saddlers wherever you can.
• Inform your insurers, they will need to know that your horse has been stolen and may provide you with recovery expenses.

Horsewatch Schemes

Many horse owners are determined to help the police crack equestrian crime. Every week more and more people decide to join horsewatch schemes, or if one is not operating in their area, set one up of their own. Similar to the neighbourhood watch schemes, horsewatch members aim to report anything suspicious and to pass on any information which comes their way. As the system grows, national networks may prove to be a major force in the fight against horse and tack thieves. So even if you do not own your own horse, you can do your bit in the fight against horse crime. Every horsewatch group is set up with the assistance of its local crime prevention officer. Each group is led by a co-ordinator who is contacted with any news about thefts or with information about stolen horses.

The Owner's Responsibilities

If you are either the owner of a horse or the person in possession of someone else's horse (the keeper) you are likely to be held responsible for its actions, whether or not you were present at the time of any incident. Where a horse has caused personal injury, certain factors will be considered which will help to determine responsibility. For instance you will have to prove that you took all reasonable care when riding or leading your horse on the road, or when leaving your horse unattended for any reason. You could be sued for negligence if the injured party could provide evidence to show that you did not in fact take all reasonable care – so take care!

You could be sued if:

• Your horse was totally out of your control when the injury occurred.
• You knew of a particular trait of your horse that was the cause of the injury – for example, you know your horse will always kick out at red buses, and in this instance the person just happened to be getting off the bus.
• It was inevitable that your horse was going to cause the damage, whether under control or not.

However, if you could prove that the other party voluntarily accepted the risk of injury then it could be deemed their own fault. For instance, did they ignore the warning to enter the field of the biting horse, only to get bitten when they did so? Every case is judged on individual merits and you would be well advised to consult a solicitor who has experience of equestrian matters.

Liabilities

When you are responsible for a horse, whether it belongs to you or someone else, you have an obligation to look after its health and welfare. Your horse's actions may have a detrimental effect on other people's property should he stray, or cause injury to other people or animals. As the person responsible for the horse at the time, you are legally responsible for any harm or damage that occurs as a result of his actions. While some people, especially like-minded equestrian owners, may overlook a stray horse on their land, if injury or damage has resulted they will be less understanding. They will be almost certain to make a claim against you, and this is where the question of responsibility arises. Most claims are made for damage to a farmer's crops or for substantial personal injury. Therefore you must regularly check fencing for any weak spots or damaged places, and keep maximum control of your horse when you are leading him to and from the field.

Crimes of Cruelty

Though there are many caring horse owners around, there are also some who are not fit to own horses, and inflict both mental and physical pain on their animals. This may be caused by ignorance, or through deliberate maliciousness. Cruelty can range from a selfish rider working his horse into the ground, to someone who tethers his horse with no water or food, causing wilful neglect. It is quite easy to assume something when you are not fully aware of the situation; for instance, the skinny horse who stands in the field with his head drooping may well have a loving owner and a medical condition which is being treated. So before jumping to any conclusions, alert the authorities; in Great Britain these are the Royal Society for the Protection of Cruelty to Animals or your local British Horse Society welfare officer. Other countries have similar organizations and making contact with them is more appropriate than interfering yourself, as you could be putting yourself in danger or alerting possible offenders. It is far better for an officer to arrive at a location and find everything in good order, than to investigate yourself and face an angry and offended horse owner who may then hold a grudge!

Index

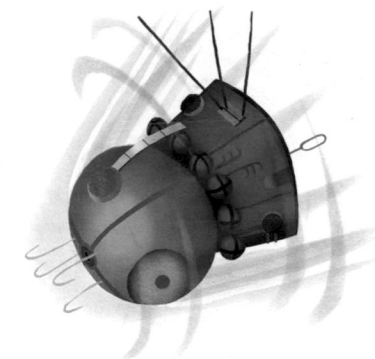

IMAGINE you were there...

WALKING ON THE MOON

 KINGFISHER

First published in 2019 by Kingfisher
an imprint of Macmillan Children's Books
20 New Wharf Road, London N1 9RR
Associated companies throughout the world
www.panmacmillan.com

Series editor: Elizabeth Yeates
Illustrations: Marc Pattenden (Advocate Art Agency)
Design: Dan Newman
Cover design: Laura Hall
Consultant: Carole Stott

ISBN: 978-0-7534-4453-5

9 8 7 6 5 4 3 2 1
1TR/0319/WKT/UG/128MA

A CIP catalogue record for this book is available from the British Library.

Printed in China

Picture credits: 6-7 bg
NASA; 8bl CBW/Alamy; 9tr
Rockatansky/iStock; 9br
Mega Pixel/Shutterstock; 12b
Historical/Getty; 23bl (waiting
on credit); 27c Henrique Alvim
Correa; 27cr Henri de Montaut;
31t NASA/JPL-Caltech; 39tl
(waiting on credit); 42 Image
Science and Analysis Laboratory,
NASA-Johnson Space Center;
54-55 NASA/GSFC/Arizona State
University; 58-59 bg 3DSculptor/
iStock; 58t jamesbenet/
iStock; 58b gremlin/iStock;
60-61 bg Yuganov Konstantin/
Shutterstock.
All other photographs NASA.

Contents

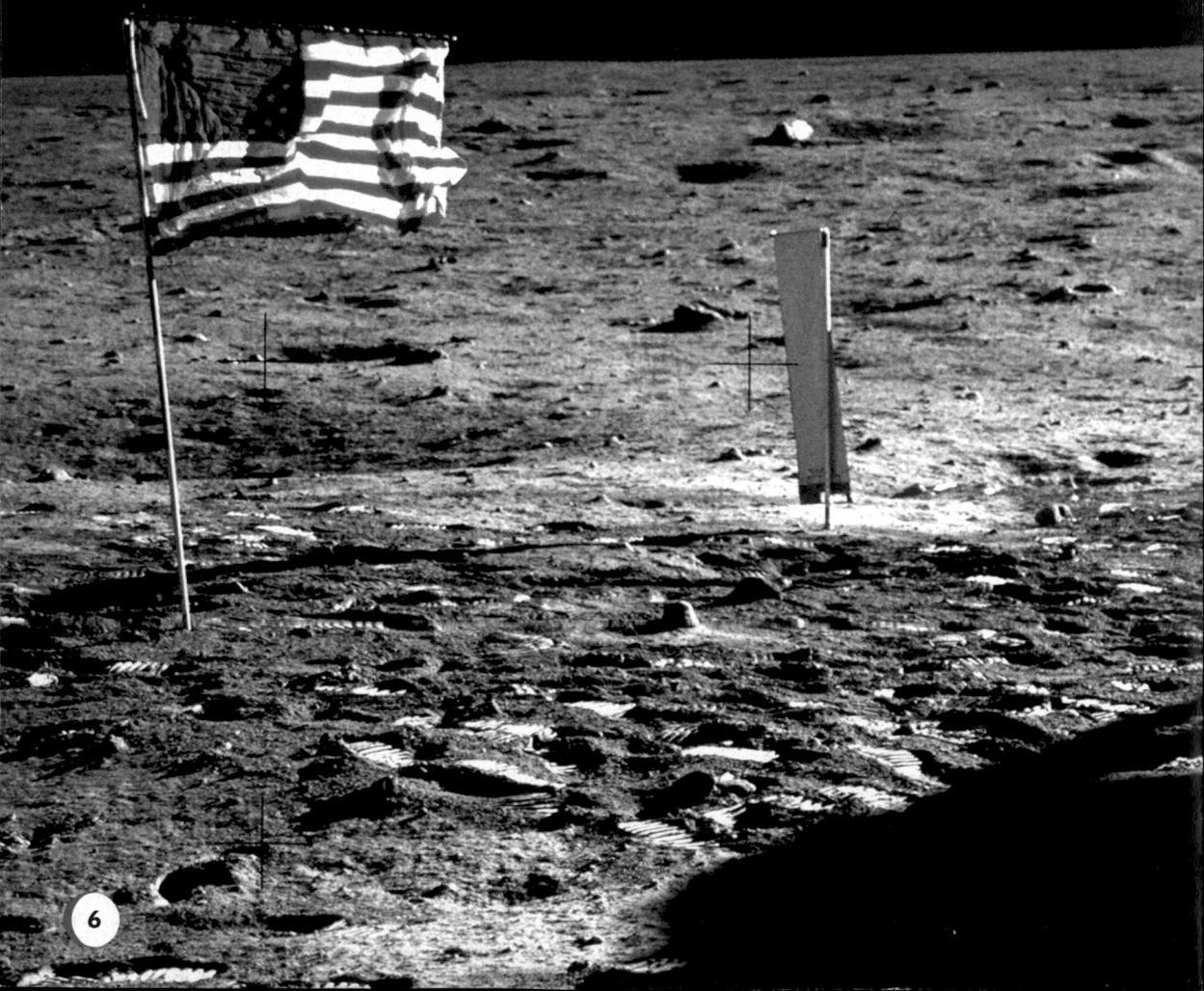

Look up at the Moon in the night sky. Now imagine being the first human to visit the Moon. Its surface is dusty and dry, and you need to wear a special spacesuit. In the distance, planet Earth looks like a blue marble. But what was it really like to walk on the Moon? And how did the astronauts get there?

On 20 July, 1969, astronauts Neil Armstrong and Buzz Aldrin became the first humans to set foot on the Moon. Back on Earth, 530 million people around the world watched on TV as Armstrong and Aldrin explored the Moon.

The Moon landing was like something from a science fiction movie – but this was real! As Neil Armstrong said when he first set foot on the Moon, "That's one small step for [a] man, one giant leap for mankind."

The Moon landing was a dangerous mission. Would the astronauts return to Earth alive?

A Changing World

The year 1969 was full of both excitement and upheaval. It was a time of protests, marches and calls for peace. People everywhere, especially young people, were standing up for what they believed in.

Women around the world were calling for equal rights with men. Black people in the United States had to struggle for equal rights, despite the Civil Rights Act of 1964, which gave them equality. Throughout the 1960s, the United States was involved in the Vietnam War, and many people protested that the American government was sending young soldiers to fight against their will. In the United Kingdom, there was continuing trouble in Northern Ireland.

But the Moon landing brought the world together.

The Vietnam War divided opinion in America.

The album Abbey Road by The Beatles was released in September 1969.

The race between the USA and the Soviet Union to land a human on the Moon was intense.

Non-violent protests against racial discrimination gained national attention.

The Vietnam War lasted from November 1955 to April 1975.

First Human in Space

The United States and the Soviet Union were rivals in world politics, and also in the race to explore space. In 1957, the Soviets launched the first satellite, called Sputnik 1, into space. The United States followed with its own satellite, Explorer. Both countries sent animals into space. The next step would be a human in space.

The Soviets achieved this on 12 April, 1961, when cosmonaut Yuri Gagarin blasted into space in Vostok 1. The flight lasted 108 minutes, making one complete orbit around Earth by travelling at speeds of 27,300 kilometres per hour (17,000 mph).

The most dangerous part of his mission was coming back to Earth. Gagarin managed to eject from the space capsule and safely parachute down to Earth, where he quickly became an international celebrity.

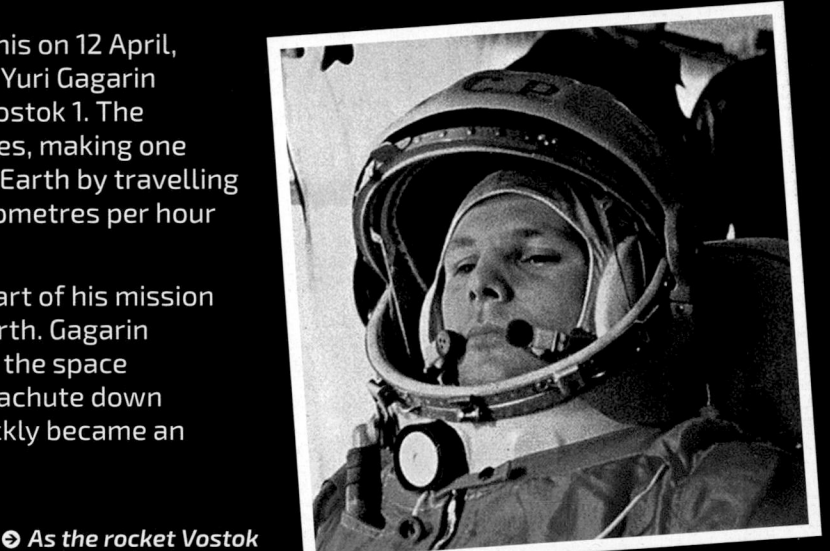

⊙ *As the rocket Vostok 1 launched, Gagarin shouted, "Let's go!"*

⊙ *Yuri Gagarin was on the front page of many newspapers around the world.*

The Huntsville Times

Feature Index

VOL. 31, NO. 21   CHICAGO DAILY NEWS SERVICE   HUNTSVILLE, ALABAMA, WEDNESDAY, APR. 12, 1961   ASSOCIATED PRESS — WIREPHOTO   45c PER WEEK

Man Enters Space

'So Close, Yet So Far,' Sighs Cape

U. S. Had Hoped For Own Launch

CAPE CANAVERAL, Fla. (AP) — The Redstone rocket which the United States had hoped would boost the first man into space stands on a launching pad here. The Soviet Union beat its firing date by at least two weeks.

"So close, yet so far," commented a technician who is helping groom the Redstone to send one of America's astronauts on a short sub-orbital flight, hopefully late this month or early in May.

"If we hadn't had those three delays last fall and on the chimp Little Joe shots this year we might have made it," the technician said.

"But you have to give the Russians scientists credit. They've accomplished a remark...

Soviet Officer Orbits Globe In 5-Ton Ship

Maximum Height Reached Reported As 188 Miles

MOSCOW (AP) — A Soviet astronaut has orbited the globe for more than an hour and returned safely to receive the plaudits of scientists and political leaders alike. Soviet announcement of the feat brought praise from President Kennedy and U. S. space experts left behind in the contest to put the first man into successful space flight.

By the Soviet account, Maj. Yuri Alekseyevich Gagarin, rode a five-ton spaceship once around the earth in an orbit taking an hour and 40 minutes. He was in the air a total of an hour and 48 minutes.

The whole sequence of events and the announcements relating to it raised a number of ...

VON BRAUN'S REACTION:

To Keep Up, U. S. ...

Hobbs Admits 1944 Slaying

A fault on re-entry caused Gagarin's space capsule to spin out of control. The capsule's temperature rose alarmingly.

Gagarin: "I was in a cloud of fire rushing towards Earth."

First spacewoman

Soviet cosmonaut Valentina Tereshkova was chosen for the space programme because of her skill as a parachute jumper. In 1963, she became the first woman in space. During her three-day mission in Vostok 6, Tereshkova orbited Earth 48 times.

The Space Race

Only 23 days after Gagarin's historic space flight, Alan Shepard became the first American in space. He flew 187 kilometres (116 miles) high and then returned to Earth in a flight lasting just over 15 minutes.

In May 1961, U.S. President John F. Kennedy declared, "I believe that this nation should commit itself to achieving the goal, before this decade is out, of landing a man on the Moon and returning him safely to Earth."

No one knew exactly how to land a man on the Moon, but they had confidence in the potential of technology. After all, the technology of their generation was already incredibly advanced compared with the past.

NASA (National Aeronautics and Space Administration), the American organization in charge of space exploration, had been set up in 1958 with the aim of expanding human knowledge of space. But now NASA focused specifically on exploring the Moon.

Alan Shepard

Astronaut Alan Shepard became an American hero when he flew to space in the Freedom 7 space capsule in 1961. Shepard returned to space in 1971 and became the fifth person to walk on the Moon. He even hit two golf balls on the Moon and watched them fly away into space.

○ *President Kennedy, his wife Jackie, and Vice President Johnson gathered to watch Alan Shepard's flight into space.*

U.S. President John F. Kennedy regularly addressed colleagues from all political parties. He never got to see a human land on the Moon, as he was assassinated in November 1963.

Space Missions

Each space mission brought NASA several steps closer to the goal of landing a human on the Moon. One of the first major advances occurred in 1962, when John Glenn became the first American to orbit Earth, travelling around three times in the Friendship 7 Mercury capsule.

Astronaut John Glenn's three orbits around Earth in 1962 lasted almost five hours, a substantial increase over NASA's previous space flights of just over 15 minutes. In 1998, Glenn travelled into space again at the age of 77 – the oldest person to take on such a mission.

⊙ John Glenn enters his Friendship 7 capsule and is ready to begin his mission.

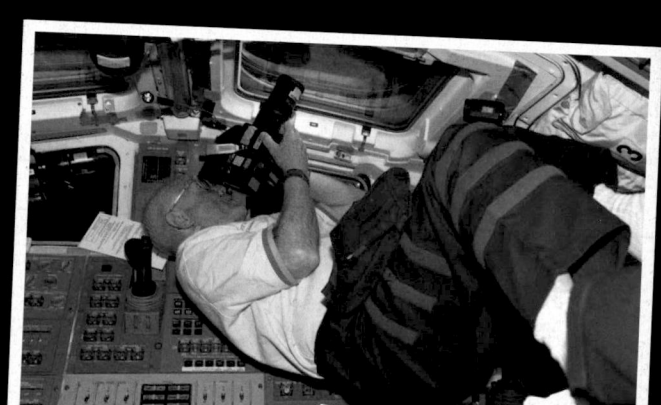

⊙ John Glenn takes photographs during his space mission in 1998.

Apollo 1

In January 1967, the Apollo 1 mission ended in tragedy when the Command Module caught fire during a pre-flight test. Astronauts Virgil Grissom, Edward White and Roger Chaffee all died. The disaster led NASA to improve safety precautions.

By 1968, the U.S. space programme had come a long way. In October of that year, Apollo 7 orbited Earth continuously for 11 days, and on Christmas Eve, Apollo 8 made the first manned orbit of the Moon.

In March 1969, NASA launched Apollo 9 into space to orbit Earth and practise various tasks, such as testing spacesuits. In May 1969, the Apollo 10 Lunar Module came within just over 15 kilometres (50,000 ft) of the Moon's surface, but didn't land.

The preparations were complete, and NASA was now ready for the big event – an Apollo mission to land humans on the Moon.

⊙ Apollo 8's view of Earth and the Moon. Images taken from space changed how people thought of our planet.

Apollo 11 Astronauts

Who would NASA choose to go to the Moon? That was a big question. NASA selected three experienced astronauts – Neil Armstrong, Buzz Aldrin and Michael Collins.

Neil Armstrong

Mission Commander Neil Armstrong was born in Ohio, USA. He was fascinated by airplanes and earned his pilot's licence at age 16 – before he could even drive a car. Later, Armstrong became a test pilot, flying high-speed aircraft into space.

↑ Aldrin, Armstrong and Collins on the day after their selection was announced to the public.

← Neil A. Armstrong, Commander; Michael Collins, Command Module Pilot; and Edwin E. Aldrin Jr., Lunar Module Pilot.

In 1962, NASA accepted Armstrong into the second class of astronauts it had ever put together. In 1966, he was command pilot for Gemini 8, where he and fellow astronaut David Scott performed the first space docking in orbit – the linking of two space vehicles. But the space vehicles began to spin uncontrollably. Armstrong regained control and was later praised for his quick thinking. He was a skilled astronaut with the qualities needed to lead the mission to the Moon.

❷ *Neil Armstrong with his wife, Janet, and two sons: Eric, who was 12 years old at the time of the Moon landing in 1969, and Mark, who was six.*

Gemini 8

On 16 March, 1966, astronauts Neil Armstrong and David Scott successfully completed their space mission. With the yellow flotation device deployed, their spacecraft landed in the ocean, where the pair awaited rescue. The green dye released on landing helped rescuers spot the craft from the air. Despite having spent almost 11 hours in space, orbiting Earth six times, both astronauts suffered more from seasickness than from their time in space.

Apollo 11 Astronauts

Buzz Aldrin

Lunar Module pilot Edwin E. "Buzz" Aldrin Jr. grew up in New Jersey, USA, and served in the Air Force, where he was awarded the Distinguished Flying Cross. He studied techniques for designing and building spacecraft and joined NASA in 1963.

His technique for docking spacecraft in orbit was crucial to the success of NASA's space programmes. In 1966, as pilot of the Gemini 12 space mission, Aldrin performed a space walk outside of the vehicle, known as extravehicular activity (EVA).

◑ *The first space selfie taken by Aldrin!*

◑ *It was Aldrin who suggested training underwater to simulate walking in space.*

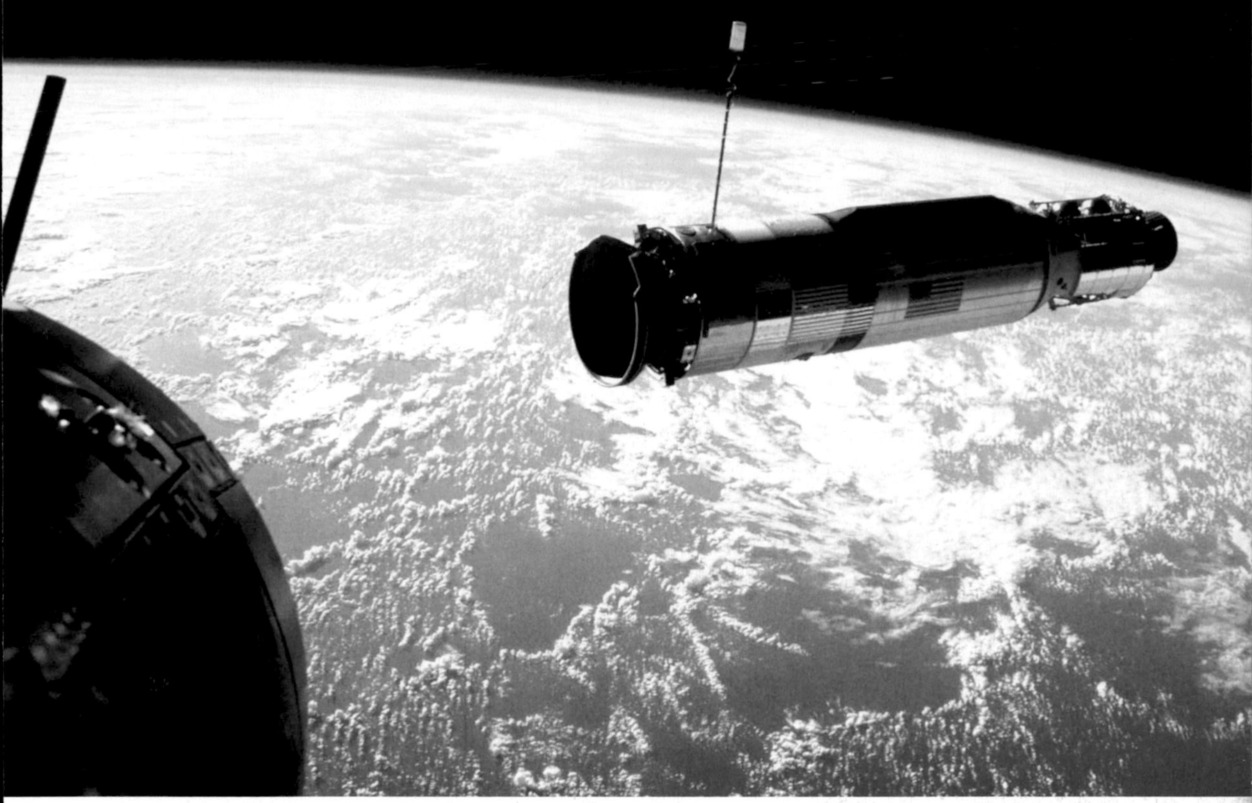

⊙ The Gemini spacecraft (left) was piloted by Michael Collins. The other craft, Agena (right), was at the same orbit approach at the same time – known as a rendezvous.

Michael Collins

Command Module pilot Michael Collins was born in Rome, Italy, but grew up in Washington, D.C., USA. He served in the United States Air Force and, like Armstrong, became a test pilot, flying fighter jets.

He was a back-up pilot for NASA's Gemini 7 mission in 1963, and pilot for Gemini 10 in 1966. During Gemini 10, Collins docked his spacecraft with two other vehicles in separate locations. He also completed two EVAs, including one particularly tricky space walk during which he recovered an important experiment from one of the other vehicles. The success of this mission added to the knowledge of human space flight.

Shooting for the Moon

It took about 400,000 people doing a wide variety of jobs to get the three Apollo 11 astronauts to the Moon. There were backup astronauts; engineers and mechanics; scientists, seamstresses, doctors and astronomers; navigators and Mission Control staff, plus managers, secretaries, cleaning and catering staff, and many, many more.

Geologists *predicted that the Moon's surface would be similar to rough, rocky craters in Arizona, USA.*

Mechanics, **welders**, **electricians** *and others built the spacecraft.*

We sewed the layers to make the spacesuits.

As engineers, we designed the spacecraft.

We were incredibly proud of our dads.

Backup astronauts *James Lovell, William Anders and Fred Haise*

Astronauts *Neil Armstrong, Buzz Aldrin and Michael Collins*

Apollo 11 Mission Patch

The astronauts' names are not on the Apollo 11 patch because NASA wanted to honour everyone involved. The bald eagle is the national symbol of the USA. It is shown landing on the Moon with an olive branch in its claws to represent peace. Earth is in the background.

I helped to develop special freeze-dried food for the astronauts to eat in space.

We were worried our husbands wouldn't come back.

We spoke to the astronauts in space from Mission Control in Houston, Texas, USA.

Air Force General **Samuel C. Phillips** *was in charge of the Apollo Manned Lunar Landing Program.*

Navy diver *who swam to meet the astronauts after splashdown in the Pacific Ocean.*

Photographer *Ralph Morse for LIFE magazine*

Spacesuits

The astronauts' spacesuits had to allow them to move around easily, while also protecting them from dangers on the Moon, such as rocks, extreme temperatures and the airless atmosphere.

NASA hired a specially trained team of seamstresses at an underwear manufacturer to make the spacesuits. Each suit had many layers made of different materials. One layer was pressurized with oxygen to allow the astronauts to breath. Some of the materials were invented specially for the spacesuits – for example, the astronauts wore a piped garment, which kept them cool. Specially developed ribbed space boots allowed the astronauts to walk on the Moon's dust and rocks.

Pressurized helmet and suit

Headset

Visor to protect against solar glare

Sunglasses pocket

Radio switch

Oxygen out

Oxygen in

Thick padded glove

Nine protective outer layers

Tubing carrying water around the cooling garment

Tough overshoe

Insulated inner boot

⊙ Neil Armstrong had a "to do" checklist sewn onto the cuff of his spacesuit.

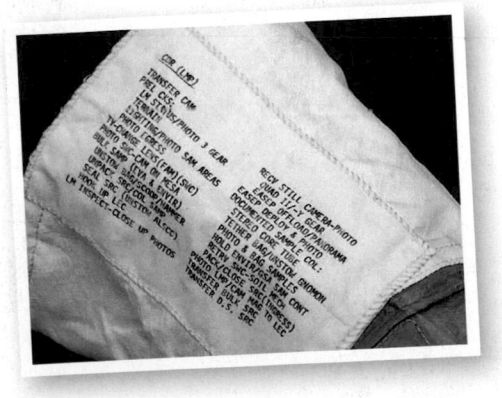

⊙ The astronauts also carried a special pack on their back containing a Portable Life Support System (PLSS), which supplied them with oxygen, water and power while they were away from their space vehicle.

Eleanor Foraker, seamstress:
"We made up each layer separately for the whole suit... Then we piled them up: one layer on top of another layer."

Spacesuit tester

The spacesuit tester was about the same size as the three astronauts, so it was his job to test the spacesuits and boots. He spent a lot of time walking on a treadmill while engineers studied how well he was able to move in different spacesuits.

Astronaut Training

How does a person prepare to go to the Moon? The astronauts trained to be in excellent physical condition, but they also practised every detail of their mission over and over again.

They practised withstanding g-forces – the increased pull of gravity that they would feel as the rocket soared swiftly out of Earth's atmosphere. (It's similar to how a really fast fairground ride feels, but much, much stronger). They also practised walking and moving around in low gravity and carrying out tasks in their new spacesuits

➔ Astronaut Neil Armstrong practised various tasks in a simulator.

➔ Buzz Aldrin practised being in weightless conditions in a specially built plane.

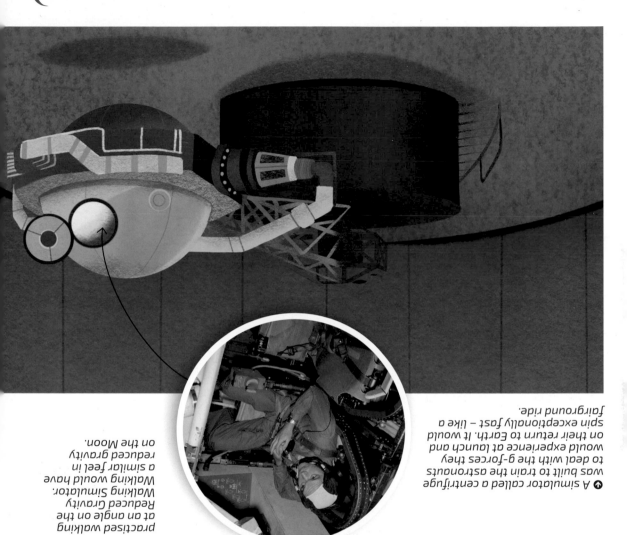

♦ A simulator called a centrifuge was built to train the astronauts to deal with the g-forces they would experience at launch and on their return to Earth. It would spin exceptionally fast – like a fairground ride.

♦ The astronauts practised walking at an angle on the Reduced Gravity Walking Simulator. Walking would have a similar feel in reduced gravity on the Moon.

The astronauts used simulators to practise flying the modules, especially for the tricky manoeuvre of docking. They carried out the experiments that they would be doing in space, and studied astronomy and geology to learn about the stars and the environment they might find on the Moon. They had to be prepared for everything.

Apollo 11 Vehicles

The engineers and technicians used everything they had learned from previous space missions when designing the Apollo 11 spacecraft.

Saturn V rocket

During previous Apollo missions Saturn V had already proved that it was powerful enough to travel beyond Earth's orbit and reach the Moon. For the Apollo 11 mission, the Saturn V rocket had three stages, each with several engines. Each stage dropped off from the rocket once its fuel was used up. At the rocket's nose sat the combined Command Module and Service Module, and the Lunar Module.

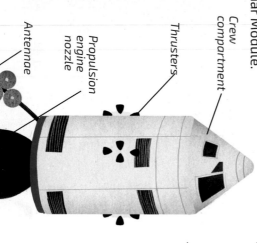

➜ The Instrument Unit is lowered into place on top of the third stage of the Saturn V rocket.

Command/ Service Modules

- Crew compartment
- Thrusters
- Propulsion engine nozzle
- Antennae

- Service Module
- Command Module

- Command Module
- Service Module
- Launch Escape System

- Lunar Module
- Instrument Unit

- Third Stage

- Second Stage

At a total height of 111 metres (363 ft), Saturn V was as tall as a 36-storey building. When fully fueled, it weighed 2.8 million kilograms (6.2 million lbs), about as much as 400 adult elephants. It had the power to launch 118,000 kilograms (130 tons) into orbit around Earth, or 45,300 kilograms (50 tons) to the Moon. That's roughly the same as launching ten buses into orbit around Earth, or four buses to the Moon. Launching three astronauts to the Moon should be no problem!

Rocket Man

The *Saturn V* rocket was developed at NASA's Marshall Space Flight Center in Alabama, USA by *Wernher von Braun*, a German-born engineer who moved to the USA after the Second World War. He was inspired to study rocketry as a child, reading the science fiction novels of Jules Verne and H.G. Wells.

Lunar Module

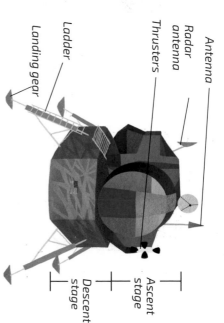

Antenna

Radar antenna

Thrusters

Ladder

Landing gear

Ascent stage

Descent stage

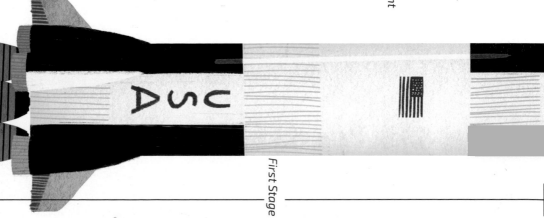

First Stage

Apollo 11 Modules

Columbia Command Module

In the Command Module (known as Columbia), the three astronauts were squeezed into roughly the space of a small car – only 3.2 metres (10.6 ft) tall by 3.9 metres (12.8 ft) at its widest point. They had very little room to move about. Special heat shields on the Command Module protected the astronauts from temperature extremes, especially when re-entering Earth's atmosphere on their return.

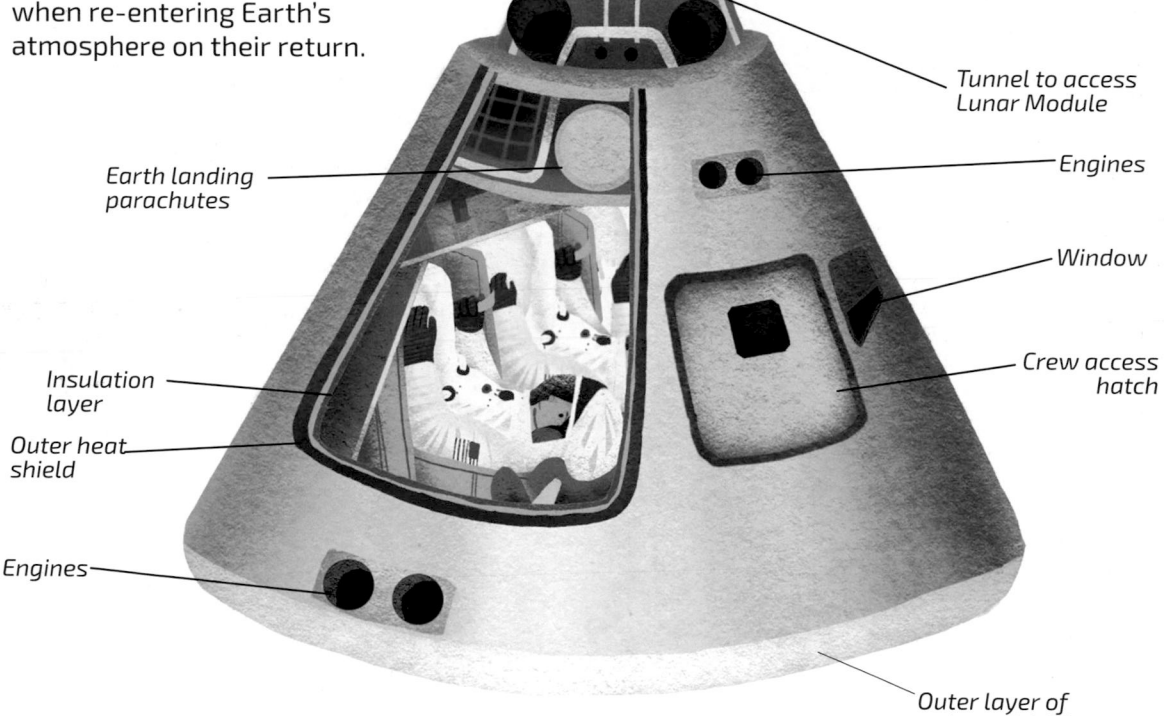

⊙ *The astronauts checked the equipment in the Command Module.*

Tunnel to access Lunar Module

Earth landing parachutes

Engines

Window

Insulation layer

Crew access hatch

Outer heat shield

Engines

Outer layer of heat shield

A Service Module providing power and fuel was attached to the Command Module for most of the mission, but was then released. Together they were called the CSM. The Command Module was the only part of the entire spacecraft to return to Earth.

Eagle Lunar Module

What sort of space vehicle could take humans to the Moon's surface and then lift off again to return to Earth? Yet another question that no one had answered before. The engineers had to use their imagination to create the Lunar Module (known as Eagle).

The Module had two sections. The lower descent stage held the landing gear, which would carry out experiments on the Moon, plus a rocket engine to descend to the Moon's surface. The upper ascent stage carried the crew and their equipment, plus a rocket engine to lift off again. At the end of the mission, the lower descent stage acted as a launch pad from the Moon and stayed there. The upper ascent stage docked with the Command Module, after which it was also dropped.

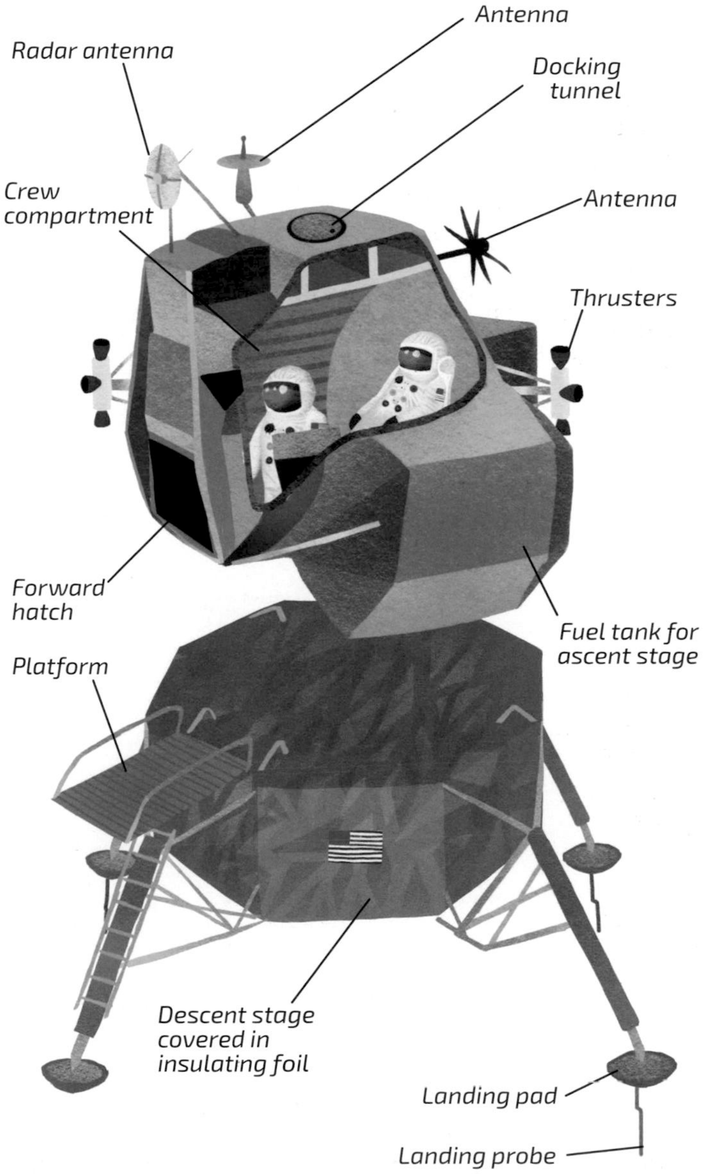

Smaller is better

The notion of a separate Lunar Module was the idea of John Houbolt, an engineer on NASA's Lunar Mission Steering Group. He had to work hard to persuade the other NASA engineers that it would be better than the enormous rocket they had in mind.

Antenna

Radar antenna

Docking tunnel

Crew compartment

Antenna

Thrusters

Forward hatch

Platform

Fuel tank for ascent stage

Descent stage covered in insulating foil

Landing pad

Landing probe

Human Computers

In the 1960s, computers were only about as powerful as today's handheld calculators. NASA relied on a group of mathematicians known as "human computers" based at Langley Research Center in Virginia, USA.

Katherine Johnson, Mary Jackson, Dorothy Vaughan and many of the other "human computers" were African-American women. Their extraordinary mathematical skill and hard work were crucial to the success of the space programme.

At a time when women and African-Americans were bravely struggling for the same rights as white men, NASA's "human computers" did not receive the credit they deserved.

⬆ *The "human computers" were initially hired to help ease the engineers' workload.*

◄ *Early machine computers weren't as reliable or efficient as the "human computers."*

◆ *During her time at NASA, Melba Roy Mouton led a group of "human computers" and became Head Computer Programmer.*

Using adding machines, pencils and paper, the mathematicians plotted graphs on the speed of the spacecraft, rotation of Earth, orbit of the Moon around Earth, and other factors in order to calculate the trajectory (flight path) of the spacecraft.

Katherine Johnson

When astronaut John Glenn was preparing for his mission to become the first American to orbit Earth in 1962, he famously only trusted the calculations of aerospace technologist Katherine Johnson, one of the "human computers".

Preparing for Launch

The Apollo 11 rocket launched from the Kennedy Space Center, on the Florida coast in America. It was named in honour of President John F. Kennedy. By the late 1960s, about 17,000 people were working at Kennedy Space Center, and as the launch date approached, engineers, technicians, scientists and other staff checked and tested every detail of the mission. Excitement was building.

The rocket and the modules had been put together at the Vehicle Assembly Building and transported to the launchpad on two giant crawler transporters.

One week before planned lift off, the Countdown Demonstration Test – the official practice launch – took place. Important challenges and lessons were learned during the test, meaning the official launch was ready. Chief of Pre-Flight Operations Raul E. "Ernie" Reyes confirmed that Apollo 11 was ready to go.

Charlie Mars, Lunar Module project engineer: "We didn't want to go home at night. We just wanted to keep going, and we couldn't wait to get up and get back in the morning – because we're going to the Moon!"

Vehicle Assembly Building

The Vehicle Assembly Building at the Kennedy Space Center had to be big enough to fit the Saturn V rocket inside. It is still one of the largest buildings in the world.

Lift-off

5... 4... 3... 2... 1... Lift-off!
On 16 July, 1969, at 9:32 a.m., at the
Kennedy Space Center in Florida,
USA the Saturn V rocket launched,
with the three astronauts inside.
The Apollo 11 space mission was
headed for the Moon!

With an enormous roar,
the Saturn V Rocket
approached the speed
of sound just one
minute into the flight.

About 500 people worked the controls in the Firing Room of the Kennedy Space Center, while about 5,000 others provided support.

Astronauts Armstrong, Aldrin and Collins sat in the Command Module at the nose of the Saturn V rocket. They soared through Earth's atmosphere and into space, dropping the first two rocket stages as they used up fuel. At 185 kilometres (115 miles) above Earth, they began orbiting, and the crew checked the spacecraft systems were performing well. Halfway through the second orbit of Earth, the last rocket stage sent them towards the Moon!

⊘ Around one million spectators on the ground watched the launch. The noise was deafening!

35

Mission Control

At Mission Control in Houston, Texas, USA, flight controllers monitored all aspects of Apollo 11's flight. Teams worked in shifts so Mission Control was fully staffed. Back-up teams were also on call.

Mission Control kept the Apollo 11 mission running as smoothly as possible. Flight controllers monitored the systems in the rocket and modules. They checked the oxygen levels and other crucial supplies for the astronauts. They ensured that the astronauts' vital statistics, such as body temperature, pulse and breathing rate, were at safe levels.

Mission Control also communicated with the astronauts. The CapCom (Capsule Communicator) relayed messages between the astronauts in space and the controllers on the ground. It was a very important job.

⊙ *Mission Control was staffed day and night throughout the mission.*

Communication to the capsule

CapCom Charlie Duke was also a trained astronaut. In 1972, he landed on the Moon as Lunar Module pilot with Apollo 16.

Life in Space

The Apollo 11 astronauts spent eight days in space.
Where did they sleep? What did they eat?
And how did they go to the toilet?

The astronauts had to be strapped in to sleep or else they would float around in the low gravity in space. It wasn't very comfortable, especially as they were squashed inside the small space modules.

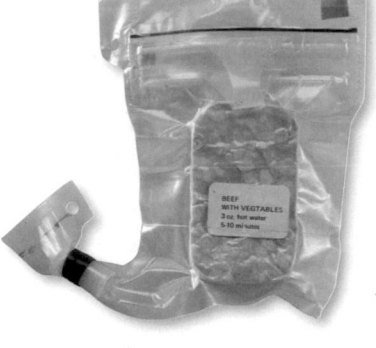

Scientists had developed freeze-dried food that was lightweight and easy to store in bags on board.

The astronauts squirted droplets of water from a special tap into the food bag and kneaded it like bread for a few minutes. Then they squeezed the food into their mouth to eat.

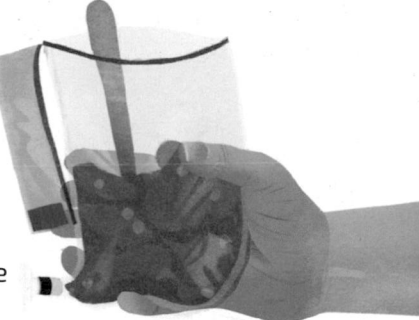

As for toilets, they don't work in space because everything would float! The astronauts used special devices that collected their body waste. They also had special nappy-style linings inside their spacesuits.

⊙ *Neil Armstrong captured this image of Buzz Aldrin during an inspection of the Lunar Module.*

Almost There...

The three stages of the rocket had dropped away some time ago. Now, the Command and Service Module (CSM), with the Lunar Module on the back, orbited the Moon twelve times, with the astronauts studying it as they flew around.

During the thirteenth orbit, the Lunar Module (Eagle) separated from the CSM, the first of many manoeuvres never attempted before. As Armstrong and Aldrin prepared to try and land the Lunar Module on the Moon, Collins continued to orbit the Moon in the CSM.

❍ *The Lunar Module separated from the Command and Service Module and headed for the Moon's surface.*

❍ *Once Armstrong and Aldrin flew off in the Lunar Module, Collins was left on his own in the CSM, in the vast emptiness of space.*

Collins: "I was alone in a way that no earthling has ever been before."

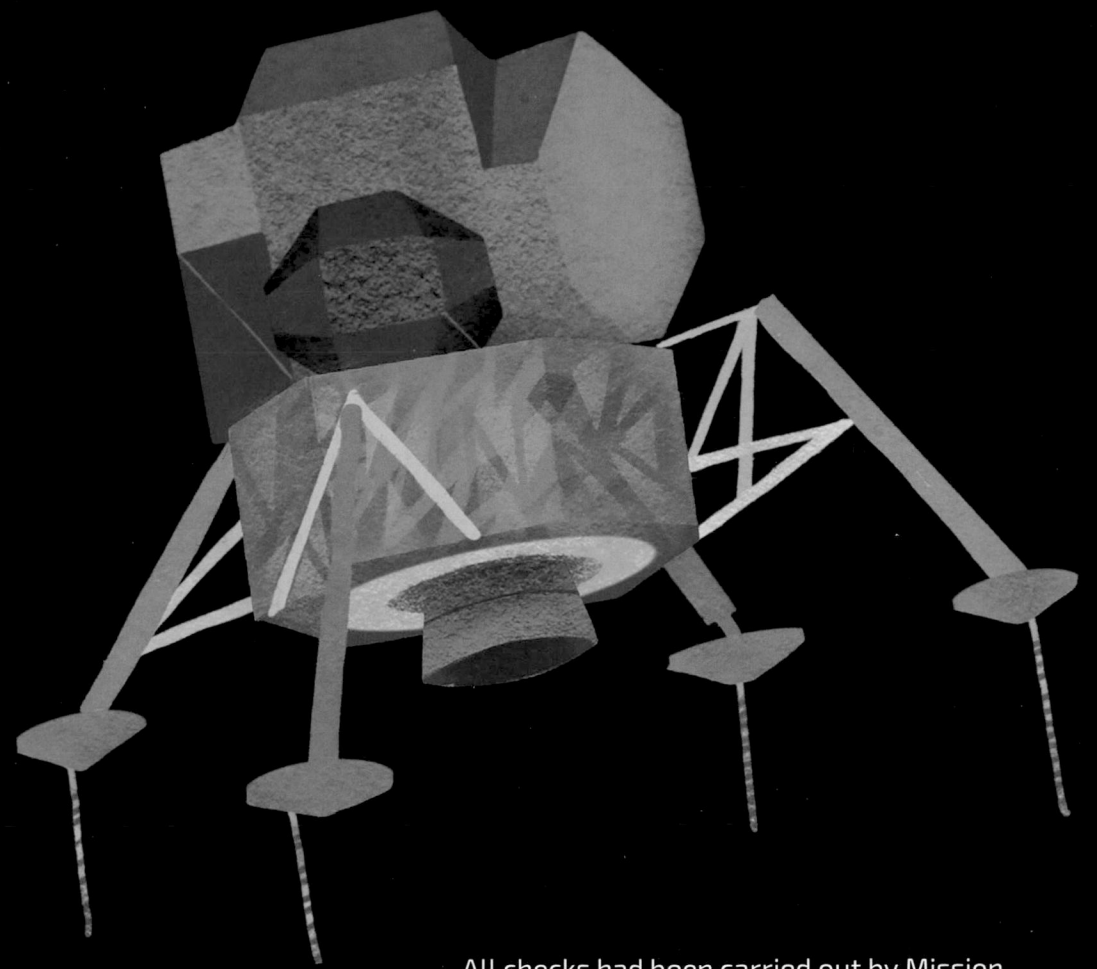

Charlie Duke at Mission Control to the Lunar Module: "You are GO to continue powered descent... Eagle, looking great. You're GO for landing..."

All checks had been carried out by Mission Control and the astronauts. With twelve minutes' worth of fuel remaining, it was time to land on the Moon. The Lunar Module began to descend to about 16 kilometres (10 miles) above the Moon. Would there be enough fuel? Would humans finally land on the Moon?

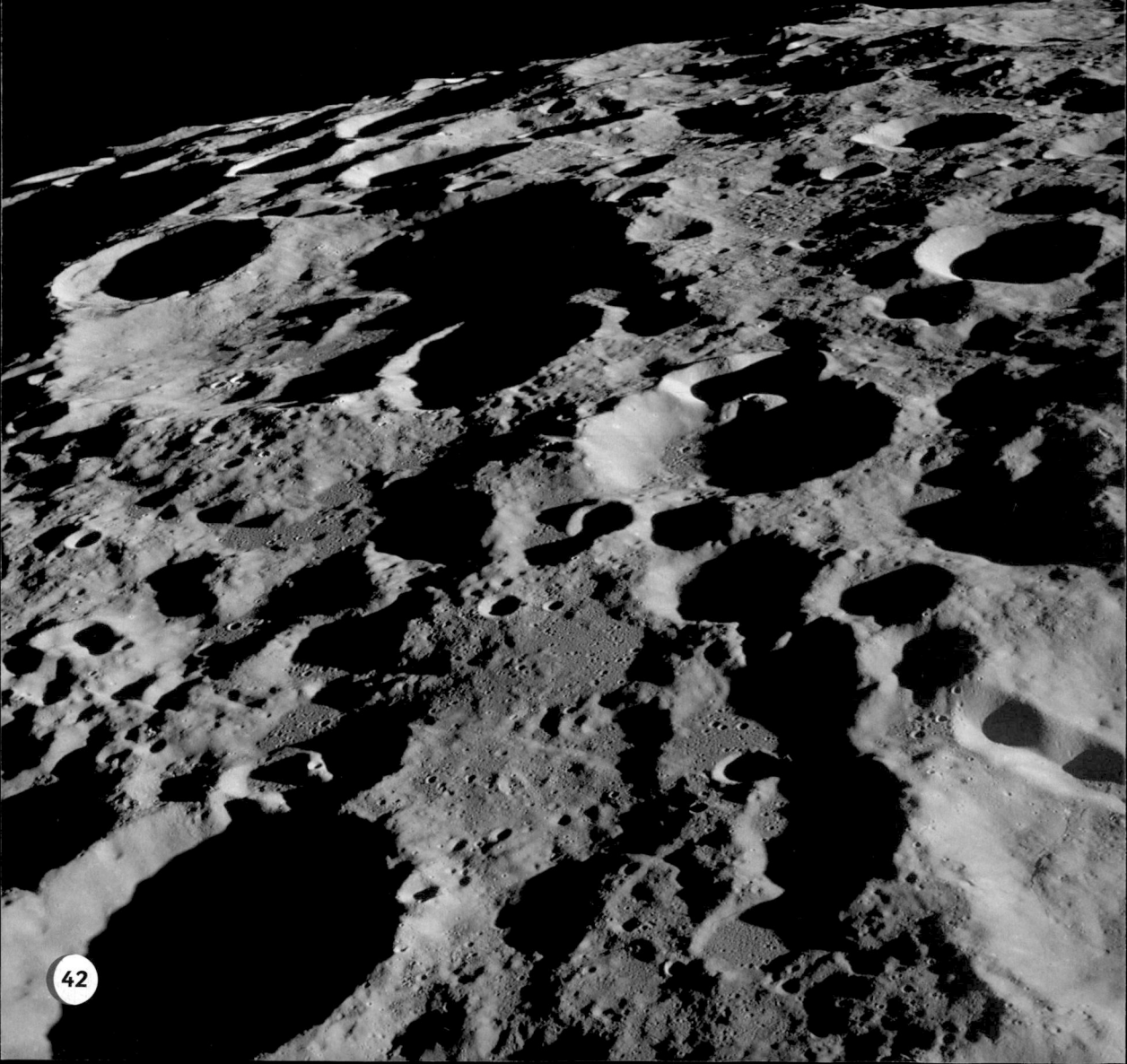

Moon Landing

As the Lunar Module descended toward the surface of the Moon, alarms sounded. Code 1202, and then a 1201! What was the problem?

At Mission Control, Steve Bales, controller for guidance and navigation, and Jack Garman, a software expert, recalled when similar alarms had gone off during a practice lift-off. Flight Director Gene Kranz had them write down what every alarm meant. Now they checked their list and realized there was no need to worry.

The Eagle has landed! Four days after lift-off, the Lunar Module finally touched down on the Moon.

Margaret Hamilton

Software engineer Margaret Hamilton was leader of the team that designed the software system on the Lunar Module. When the alarms sounded, the software was able to prioritize tasks so that Apollo 11 could continue its mission.

Dealing with the alarms had used up time and precious fuel. The astronauts had to land quickly or the Lunar Module would run out of fuel and crash onto the Moon's surface.

But landing wasn't easy. There was a crater and a field of boulders in the way. With less than 30 seconds of fuel left, Armstrong landed the Lunar Module safely on the Moon in a location known as Tranquility Base.

Armstrong: "Tranquility Base here. The Eagle has landed."

Mission Control: "Roger, Tranquility. Be advised there's lots of smiling faces in this room, and all over the world."

Armstrong: "There are two of them up here."

Collins: "And don't forget one in the Command Module."

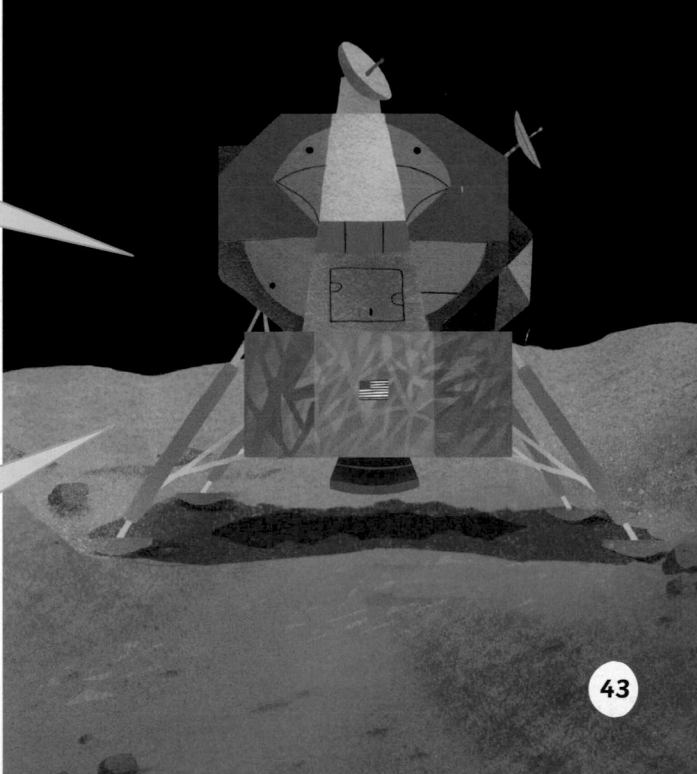

Moon Walk

Armstrong and Aldrin were so eager to explore the Moon that they skipped their scheduled rest. Instead, they prepared their portable life support backpacks and other equipment needed for their Moon walks. Then Aldrin helped Armstrong manoeuvre through the hatch of the Lunar Module and onto the ladder.

As he climbed down the ladder, Armstrong pulled the cord to activate the TV camera mounted on the outside of the Lunar Module. With the world watching, he jumped from the last rung of the ladder onto the surface of the Moon.

Armstrong: "That's one small step for [a] man, one giant leap for mankind."

◐ Aldrin leaving the Lunar Module, photographed by Armstrong.

◑ TV footage of Armstrong stepping onto the Moon.

Aldrin: "The surface is fine and powdery... I can kick it up loosely with my toe."

◐ Buzz Aldrin took photographs of his footprints on the Moon's talcum-like surface.

Twenty minutes later, Aldrin also stepped onto the Moon. The two astronauts walked and jumped around in low gravity. Aldrin called the Moon "magnificent desolation," meaning that it was beautiful, but lifeless.

Working on the Moon

One of the astronauts' main tasks was to take photos and film footage of the Moon. Armstrong took most of the photographs, so the pictures were mainly of Aldrin.

Armstrong and Aldrin collected more than 21 kilograms (47 lb) of rocks and other samples from the Moon. They conducted experiments, including one on Moonquakes and another on wind from the Sun. They also set up Laser Ranging Retroreflectors, which would help measure the distance between Earth and the Moon by reflecting lasers sent from large telescopes on Earth.

Armstrong and Aldrin spent about two and half hours on the Moon. They left behind an American flag, goodwill messages from 73 different countries, medallions honouring the Apollo 1 astronauts and Soviet cosmonauts who had died on space missions, and a plaque commemorating their visit to the Moon.

○ *Aldrin conducted several experiments.*

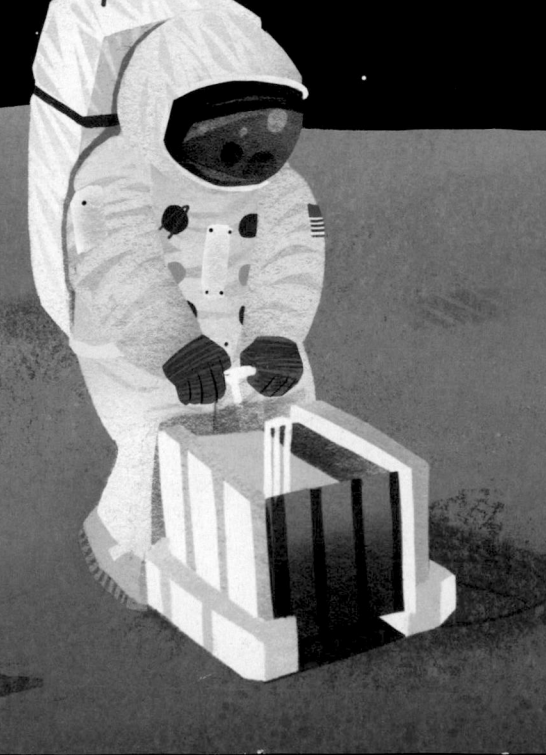

⬆ *A photograph showing Aldrin, the Lunar Module and equipment used to take measurements and collect samples.*

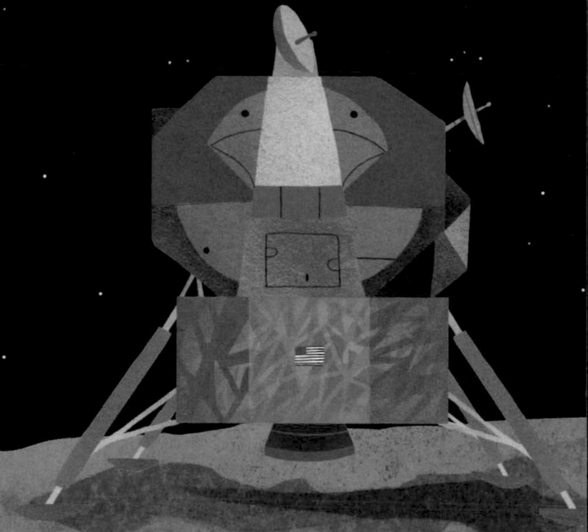

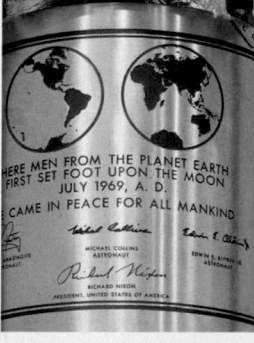

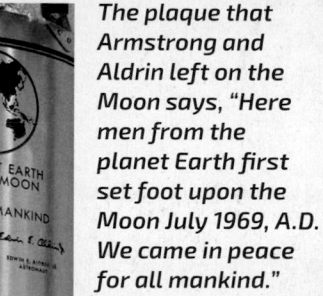

The plaque that Armstrong and Aldrin left on the Moon says, "Here men from the planet Earth first set foot upon the Moon July 1969, A.D. We came in peace for all mankind."

The World Watched

About 530 million people around the world watched the Moon walks on TV. Enormous satellite dishes in the Australian outback received signals from the television camera on the Moon. The TV signals were relayed to the city of Sydney, Australia, and then to Mission Control in Texas, USA, and then around the world.

In most of the United States, it was late at night. People stayed up so they wouldn't miss the Moon walk, and many woke their children to witness the historic event. Some people gathered to watch together. In New York City, a "moon-in" event was held in Central Park, where people watched the events live on large screens.

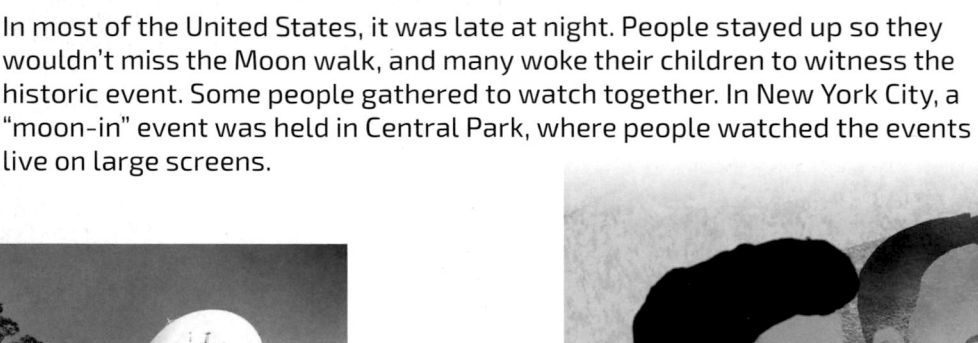

◐ *Honeysuckle Creek, Australia, was the first site to receive signals from the Moon and relay them to the viewers watching.*

Expert reporting

Astronomer Sir Patrick Moore reported on the Moon landing. He was an expert in mapping the Moon, and NASA used his research to prepare for Apollo 11.

In Europe, it was early morning of the next day. Teachers brought TV sets into classrooms to watch with their students. How amazing that people were really walking on the Moon – that big rock in space that we see in the night sky!

◑ The live TV pictures were in black and white and were blurry. Only later would the world see colour ones when the astronauts' photographs were revealed.

Back to Earth

It was time for Armstrong and Aldrin to rejoin Collins in the Command and Service Module. This was one of the trickiest parts of the mission. U.S. President Nixon had a speech prepared in case the astronauts didn't make it home.

Armstrong and Aldrin fired up the ascent stage of the Lunar Module and lifted off. Exactly as planned, they docked with the CSM as it flew past. The Lunar Module was disconnected once all of the three astronauts were safely inside the Command Module. The Service Module was then released. The 400,000-kilometre (250,000-mile) journey back to Earth had begun.

◗ *Back in the Lunar Module, Aldrin and Armstrong are tired, but elated.*

◗ *Michael Collins (inside the Command Module) took this photograph of the Lunar Module just before it docked with the CSM.*

The hardest and most dangerous part of the return journey was re-entering Earth's atmosphere. At re-entry, they were travelling at more than 11,000 metres (36,000 ft) per second. A special heat shield on the Command Module protected them from the 2,700°C (5,000°F) heat. Their mission to the Moon and back was almost over.

Splashdown

The Command Module was on target for splashdown in the Pacific Ocean. At about 3,000 metres (10,000 ft) above the ocean, specially designed parachutes opened and the Command Module drifted down into the water. Recovery helicopters flew over from the nearby USS Hornet aircraft carrier. The astronauts had made it back to Earth.

We're OK!

John Wolfram was one of four divers from the U.S. Navy who swam out to anchor the Command Module after splashdown. He said, "I looked in the hatch window to see if the astronauts were OK. They smiled and gave me a thumbs-up."

◀ After splashdown, the now famous Command Module was put on display in the National Air and Space Museum, in Washington, D.C., USA.

The astronauts were immediately put into quarantine away from anyone else, even their families, so they wouldn't spread any unknown germs.

After almost a month in quarantine, Armstrong, Aldrin and Collins were finally able to join the world's celebrations of the Moon landing. There were parades, a meeting with the U.S. president, and a lot of interviews. Everyone wanted to hear their stories and experiences.

Apollo 11 facts

Departure: 16 July, 1969

Arrival on the Moon: 20 July, 1969

Moon walk (EVA): 2 hours, 30 minutes

Total time on the Moon: 21 hours, 36 minutes

Return to Earth: 24 July, 1969

Duration of mission: 8 days, 3 hours, 18 minutes, 35 seconds

Total distance: 1.53 million kilometres (953,054 miles)

Amazing Memories

Do you know anyone who remembers watching the astronauts land on the Moon? Here are a few memories from those who were watching from all over the world.

Molly Wolfe, Yorkshire
"I was 12 years old when I watched the Moon landing from the sofa in my grandmother's living room. We were watching on television and I remember clearly the beautiful vision of Earth from the Moon and thinking it was something magical. When Armstrong stepped out and did the funny Moon walk, it felt like sci-fi! I also recall thinking it was quite funny that they put up the flag on such an empty landscape."

Bill Coon, Minnesota, USA
"I was 17 and a little nervous about the future. That summer, we had a meeting of the school council at the home of one of our teachers. We were all discussing ideas for the following school year when suddenly we stared in amazement at the small TV screen. Science fiction melded into reality right before our eyes. Humans were walking on the Moon! Anything now seemed possible and the future became more exciting than scary. The Moon landing represented hope."

Mark Leonard, East Anglia
"I was 8. What I remember is hearing one lady in our village say that she thought the Moon wasn't as bright since the astronauts had landed, and she was really annoyed about that!"

Enrique A. Farrarons, Philippines
"I was 20 when I watched the Moon landing. I immediately thought, "When can I go to the Moon"? I also wondered where humans would go next. After all, there's a whole universe out there."

Iris Purcell, New York City, USA
"I wondered if the Moon landing had been faked. At 24, I had been protesting against the Vietnam War, and I didn't trust the American government. I was among a group of skeptics who thought that the Moon landing might have been a hoax to boost morale in the country."

55

Space Technology

Did you know that some everyday items that we now take for granted came about as a result of the Apollo 11 mission to the Moon?

These are just a few of the advances made to everyday life, thanks to Apollo 11.

Cordless power tools were first invented so the astronauts could drill for samples on the Moon.

Modern computer chips that we use in mobile phones and other devices were developed using technology from the computer circuits on the Apollo modules.

When you're running and jumping around in your trainers, imagine the astronauts doing the same thing in their space boots! Modern athletic shoes use cushioned soles that were originally developed for the space boots worn by Armstrong and Aldrin to walk on the Moon.

A Future in Space

Humans have continued to explore space. In 2019, China landed a rover on the side of the Moon that never faces Earth – the first spacecraft ever to do so.

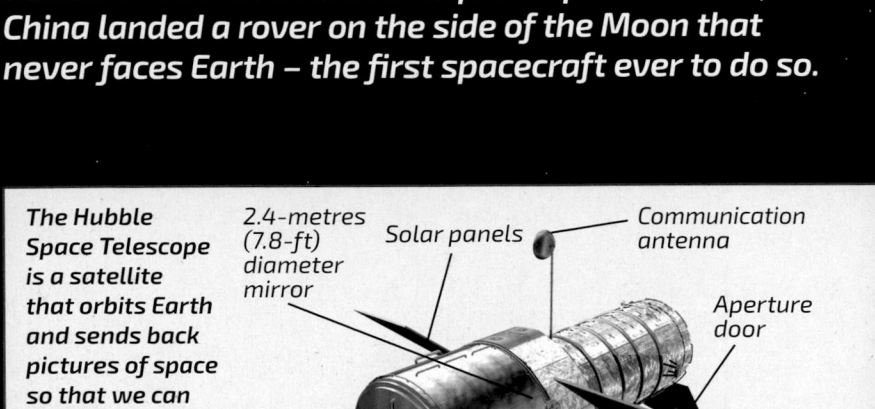

The Hubble Space Telescope is a satellite that orbits Earth and sends back pictures of space so that we can see more of the extraordinary world that lies beyond our planet.

2.4-metres (7.8-ft) diameter mirror

Solar panels

Communication antenna

Aperture door

Cameras and instruments

Computers and batteries

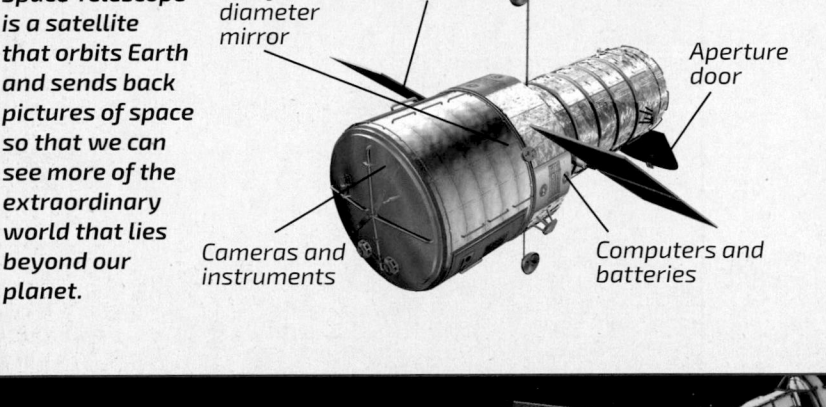

Robotic devices called probes are also sent to explore space. These probes can withstand the conditions without risking human life. One such probe is the Mars rover Curiosity, which explores the surface of Mars, the closest planet to Earth.

The International Space Station has been orbiting Earth since 1998. Astronauts stay on the space station for months at a time to conduct experiments.

But is living in space a possibility? Some entrepreneurs believe that humans should become an "interplanetary species" and live on different planets, not just Earth. They even have plans for a space colony on Mars. What do you think?

Do You Have What It Takes?

Some important qualities when working in space exploration are curiosity and enthusiasm, the ability to work well with a team, and the persistence to keep trying. Take this quiz to find out about some more qualities needed for different jobs involved in space exploration.

1 Which do you prefer?
  a Going on a school field trip
  b Organizing a group project
  c Building a model rocket
  d Doing a science experiment

2 At school, do you usually:
  a Listen closely and follow instructions
  b Try to do several things at the same time
  c Sometimes come up with unusual ideas
  d Ask a lot of questions

3 Which is your idea of fun?
  a Exploring a new place
  b Playing a computer game
  c Drawing a picture of a race car
  d Going to a science museum

4 Which word best describes you?
  a Adventurous
  b Organized
  c Creative
  d Inquisitive

If you've answered mostly . . .

a You love adventures and exploring new places. You're also brave and physically fit. Why not become an astronaut and explore space? You'll need to follow instructions from Mission Control, but at the same time, you've got to be resourceful and quick-thinking so you can solve any problems that occur in space.

b You're good at organizing and working on different things at the same time, but you also have a good eye for detail. You have an air of authority, meaning that people pay attention to what you say. That's important for someone working in Mission Control. How about it?

c You like vehicles and building things and knowing how things work. Would you like to design and build spacecraft and space probes? You'll need to be practical with good technical knowledge, and have the imagination to create spacecraft and probes suitable for exploring different places in space.

d The more you learn about the universe, the more you realize there is to learn. You're focused, precise and patient. You're also good at finding links between ideas. You could be a space scientist, thinking up experiments for the astronauts to do in space and then analyzing the results.

61

Glossary

Atmosphere The layer of gases that surround Earth and are held there by gravity. Earth's atmosphere is made up of nitrogen, oxygen, argon, carbon dioxide and small traces of other gases.

Command Module Also known as Columbia. The part of the Apollo 11 spacecraft where the astronauts lived. This part of the spacecraft returned to Earth with the astronauts inside. It had special heat shields to protect the astronauts from high temperatures.

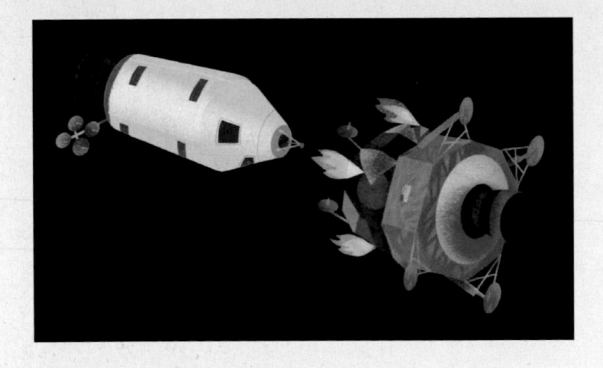

Docking When two separate space vehicles link together in flight. This is a tricky manoeuvre, as it requires the vehicles to find each other in space and get close enough to join up.

Extravehicular Activity (EVA) Activity that happens outside of the spacecraft, such as a spacewalk.

G-force An increased pull of gravity that astrounauts feel when they are launched out of Earth's atmosphere.

It's similar to how it feels on a rollercoaster, but much stronger.

Gravity The force that pulls objects towards each other. It keeps the planets in orbit around the Sun and keeps people and other objects grounded on Earth. The Moon has very low gravity, so astronauts have to learn how to walk and move around in reduced gravity conditions.

Hubble Space Telescope (HST) A space telescope above Earth's atmosphere. It completes a full orbit of Earth every 97 minutes, sending images of planets, stars and galaxies back to scientists and astronomers on Earth.

International Space Station (ISS) A spacecraft orbiting Earth. Launched in 1998, astronauts live and work on the ISS, carrying out tests and research.

Laser Ranging Retroreflectors Equipment used to measure the distance between the Earth and the Moon. Lasers on the Earth were pointed at retroreflectors on the Moon and the distance between the two can then be calculated.

Lunar Module Also known as the Eagle. A space vehicle used in the Apollo 11 mission. Neil Armstrong and Buzz Aldrin landed the Lunar Module on the Moon in July 1969.

Mission Control A facility based on Earth that monitors all aspects of a space mission.

Moonquake A shaking sensation (a quake) that occurs on the Moon. Moonquakes last longer but are weaker than earthquakes.

NASA National Aeronautics and Space Administration. An American organization in charge of space exploration. Founded in 1958, NASA was responsible for the first manned mission to the Moon, the Apollo 11.

Orbit The circular path an object takes in space around another object. For example, Earth is in orbit around the Sun, and the Moon is in orbit around Earth.

Portable Life Support System (PLSS) A special pack astronauts carried on their back,

which supplied them with oxygen, water and power when they were away from their space vehicle.

Probes An unmanned spacecraft that travels through space to collect information. Sputnik 1 was the first probe in space.

Rendezvous When two spacecraft are in the same orbit at the same time and come within a very close distance of each other.

Satellite A satellite is an object that is in orbit. The Moon is a natural satellite, but sometimes artificial satellites are launched into space to do a certain job, such as taking and sending pictures and mapping planets.

Service Module The part of the Apollo 11 spacecraft that provided power, storage and other important functions needed on the mission. It was connected to the Command Module and was released before landing and did not return to Earth.

Trajectory The path an object takes through space.

Index